Heinemann Short Stories
One

My World

Poetry Anthologies edited by Rhodri Jones

Themes Series
Men and Beasts
Conflict

Preludes Series
Families
Work and Play
Weathers
Five Senses

Heinemann Short Stories
One

My World

Selected and edited by Rhodri Jones
Headmaster of John Kelly Boys' High School, Brent

Heinemann Educational Books
LONDON

Heinemann Educational Books Ltd
22 Bedford Square, London WC1B 3HH
LONDON EDINBURGH MELBOURNE AUCKLAND
SINGAPORE KUALA LUMPUR NEW DELHI
IBADAN NAIROBI JOHANNESBURG
PORTSMOUTH (NH) KINGSTON

Cover design and photography by Chris Gilbert

First published 1980

Reprinted 1981, 1982, 1985, 1986, 1987

British Library Cataloguing in Publication Data

Heinemann short stories.
 Book 1: My world
 1. Short stories, English
 I. Jones, Rhodri
 823'.9'1FS   PR1309.S5

 ISBN 0–435–13490–6

Printed and bound in Hong Kong by
Dah Hua Company Ltd

Contents

Acknowledgements

The editor and publishers wish to thank the following for permission to reproduce copyright material:
Penguin Books for 'Casey and the Damp Squibs' from *Tommy Mac* by Margaret Stuart Barry (Longman Young Books 1972) © Margaret Stuart Barry 1972, and for 'What the Neighbours Did' from *What the Neighbours Did and Other Stories* by Philippa Pearce (Longman Young Books 1972) © Philippa Pearce, 1967, 1972; George Harrap for 'A Bit of Bread and Jam' from *The Goalkeeper's Revenge* by Bill Naughton; Jonathan Cape for 'The Apple of Trouble' from *A Small Pinch of Weather* by Joan Aiken; J. M. Dent & Sons and the Trustees for the Copyrights of the late Dylan Thomas for 'Memories of Christmas' from *Quite Early One Morning* by Dylan Thomas; André Deutsch for 'Enchanted Alley' from *Cricket on the Road* by Michael Anthony; Hamish Hamilton and A. D. Peters for 'The Idealist' from *Stories of Frank O'Connor* by Frank O'Connor; Hamish Hamilton for 'The Night the Ghost Got In' from *Vintage Thurber* © the Copyright Collection.

Illustrations

Introduction

The short stories in this collection are intended primarily to be read for entertainment and pleasure. They should particularly interest pupils in the first year of the secondary school.

The stories deal with subjects that should involve you – things like friends and enemies, games and hobbies, adventures and discoveries, families and neighbours. By reading, you can find out more about your world and how your experiences and feelings compare with those of other people of your age. You can also find out more about how writers organise their ideas and experiences into the shape of a story and how they use words to bring these ideas and experiences vividly alive. To help you do this, there are notes and suggestions for discussion and writing on each story at the end of the volume.

They may encourage you to go on and write your own stories. If you enjoy a story here by a particular writer, try to read more stories or novels by him or her: suggestions for titles to look for are also given at the end.

Casey and the Damp Squibs

MARGARET STUART BARRY

'We need a terrific lot of money for fireworks this year,' announced Tommy Mac. 'They've gone up something shocking.'

'Well, we haven't *got* a lot, have we?' said Chai.

'And we aren't likely to get a lot, are we?' added Raff.

'I've had my pocket money stopped,' sighed Nessy.

'Why's that then?' asked Tommy.

Nessy grinned widely and scratched his head. 'That Monday I sagged school, Mrs Nosey Lunt saw me down by the iron bridge and she told on me.'

'Oh well, you're daft!' snorted Tommy. 'You should've gone farther off.'

'I wonder if Casey's got much,' said Raff. 'He says he has.'

'Yes, but he's a liar, isn't he, so maybe he has and maybe he hasn't,' Tommy sneered.

'I know!' interrupted Raff. 'We'll all do jobs at home, and work hard, and not get on anyone's nerves, and . . .'

'That's no good,' scoffed Tommy, 'we'd never get enough. The cheapest rocket costs forty pence and them cheap ones fizzle out six inches above the ground.'

The boys looked gloomy. They wouldn't have minded too much if only they could have been sure that Casey's gang wasn't going to out-sparkle or out-bang them.

They drifted into the local snack bar, adopting the manner of cowboys mozeying into their local saloon.

'Four Cokes, and line 'em up,' said Tommy.

'What?' asked the girl behind the counter.

'Four Cokes. Are you deaf or something?'

'She's got rubber lugs!' choked Raff.

'Hey, you, are you speaking to me? I don't have to serve you scruff if I don't want to.'

'You do, girl,' said Tommy. 'Your boss is a proper old skinter – isn't he fellas?'

'Worst old skinter round here,' agreed the boys loyally.

'So,' continued Tommy, enjoying this bit of mickey-taking, 'if he was to find out you turned good money away – money what's the same as anyone else's – he'd get dead stroppy with *you*.'

The girl was new at the job and unaccustomed to the gang. She was half afraid that what the gang had said might be true. So she thumped four Cokes on to the counter – making sure to slop a little out of each. Tommy reckoned that was fair do's, but stared at the girl long enough to make her blink.

'We've just wasted the price of four bangers,' observed Chai.

'Not wasted,' scolded Tommy. 'I need a drink to think.' He'd heard Stevey saying that often.

'Well,' grunted Raff, 'I can still only think of doing jobs, and working hard . . .'

'I've got it!' yelled Tommy. 'Why didn't I think of it before?'

'Think of what?' cried the gang.

'Going into business!' exclaimed Tommy.

'Business?'

'Of course! Gosh, it was so easy! Ma Carney does it and Darky Cohen and Ritzy O'Riley. *Thousands* of them do it.'

'Yes, and they don't have any other job, do they!' gasped Raff.

'And they pay their rents and live off it, don't they!' said Chai.

'And live and eat and everything!' agreed Tommy.

'But what do they sell?' put in Raff, who thought someone ought to be sensible.

The other three regarded him irritably.

'Darky Cohen sells dogs.'

'That's easy,' said Tommy. 'We just go to the dogs' home and offer to sell some of their dogs for them. They should be jolly glad to let us have a few. It would save a lot of dogs' lives because they only have to kill'm when they've got too many.'

Raff wasn't sure they'd be allowed to have even a few dogs. 'Supposing we didn't sell them all in one day,' he said, 'we'd be lumbered with them.'

3

This was true. Tommy could imagine that his mother would not be very pleased if he brought half a dozen dogs home with him. Count and Dracula might not be very pleased either. Count and Dracula were both good fighters, and might easily eat all the profits.

'Well then,' he said, 'what does Ma Carney sell?'

'Junk,' said Chai.

'Exactly, junk, and our house is already full of that.'

'And ours,' chorused the others.

It was a nuisance having to go to school. It wasted a great many valuable business hours. By the time they were let out, their brains were tired from concentrating on useless sums and on writing stupid poems about stupid autumn leaves; stupid because the only objects over ten feet tall in *their* street were lamp posts which didn't have 'leaves of yellow, gold and brown, fluttering gently, gently down,' but only broken light bulbs.

'Where *she* lives they've got trees,' said Nessy.

'Who?' asked Tommy.

'Miss Peterson.'

'Well, *she* ought to write about them, then, and leave us in peace,' decided Tommy.

Wearily, the boys collapsed in Nessy's front room. Nessy's father was on night shift and his mother was out playing bingo. The rest didn't count; the older ones were outside playing in the street and the others were in bed. It was a funny house, Tommy thought; full of the sort of things he didn't have in his. Full was not quite the right word for there was actually very little furniture. There was a large table and enough chairs round it to seat the O'Shaughnessy family. And there was a sink, and a cooker, and a record player. But there were also strange things like African drums, and masks pinned to the walls, and milk bottles on the dresser crammed with plants that Tommy had never seen anywhere else.

'The first thing,' he said, when he had finished staring, 'is to put up our stall where nobody knows us.'

'But why not in Fish Street or Paradise Way?' asked Raff.

'Because Casey'll see it,' said Tommy.

4

Neither Casey and his gang nor Tommy Mac and his ever wandered more than about ten streets away from their own, except to go to town or to the park or on a special excursion to visit relatives. As far as they were concerned, other areas of the city were like foreign countries. Therefore it wasn't very difficult to find a place for their stall quite near to home. The place they eventually found was in a street lined with partially demolished houses.

'This is jolly handy!' exclaimed Tommy. 'Look at all them planks and bricks.'

'What'll we do with them?' asked Nessy.

'Make a counter, of course.'

'Oh yes!' cried Nessy. 'And we could build a hut to sit in for when it rains.'

'With seats in it,' said Chai.

The boys marvelled at the fact that they had never before thought of going into business and also at the fact that they had never been in this particular street which was so full of promise and unexplored rubbish.

'And another thing, d'you know what?' added Tommy. 'We could go into the scrap business, too. Look at all those drain-pipes and bed irons and old cookers. Gosh! I read once where there was this fella who became a millionaire just because he bothered picking all this sort of stuff up.'

Almost drunk with delight and ambition, the boys wended their way home to supper. Each of them owned a mother who expected that he should show up at meal times, and who thought of things like baked beans and toast and dishes and cookers but never of becoming a millionaire.

The following day was Saturday, the most precious day of the week. Armed with enough junk to fill Woolworths from the front door to the back, the boys set off for their new place, which they had named Jericho. Nessy and Chai lugged the go-cart whilst Tommy and Raff kept an eye skinned for Casey and his lot. 'Probably still soaking in bed,' observed Tommy exhilarated.

In five minutes, the boys had erected a counter and covered it with junk. Nessy, in the background, was taking longer to

5

construct a shelter. He had found an old painting and was busily trying to fix it into the brickwork.

'Makes it look like an office,' he explained.

It was amazing, Nessy thought, the amount of useful objects people leave behind. He had found two kitchen chairs, a bookcase with all the shelves still intact, and a suitcase with only one small hole in a corner.

'Hey Ness, that's gear!' praised Tommy. 'Ritzy O'Reilly uses a suitcase like that when he's packing up.'

By now it was ten o'clock. A drove of housewives with large shopping bags was bearing down the street. Most of them ignored the boys, but one fat woman came across to the stall, examined it critically, and asked, 'How much's those?'

'The shoes?' asked Tommy. 'Five pence.'

'L'avem for three,' said the fat woman, her face expressionless.

'All right,' Tommy agreed, and business began.

'You should've stuck to five,' said Chai.

'You just don't know about business,' said Tommy scornfully. 'You pretends to want twice as much – make your tickets dearer, like – then one gets the price you really expected.'

'What?' said Chai.

'Never mind, wack,' said Tommy wearily.

At the end of the day the gang had made fifty-five pence. They could hardly believe it.

Sunday, they all agreed, was not a good day for trading, so it was Monday after school when the boys reassembled at Jericho. Tommy had spent Sunday afternoon making treacle toffee. This was one thing he was good at. Charlie had got at the toffee and eaten quite a lot, and Mags and Kate a bit more. Tommy himself had eaten a certain amount but there was still a good deal left. He shared it out into empty margarine containers and arranged them temptingly on the stall.

That day several women came straight up to the stall. They were mainly interested in the clothes and none of them would pay the prices the boys asked. This was really not very surprising as Tommy had priced his father's old raincoat at two pounds fifty, which was not far off the original price.

6

'I'll give yer twenty-five pence for it,' a woman offered.

'Twenty-five!' This time Tommy was outraged. 'We're not running this business for charity, you know. It's not your bloomin' W.R.V.S. or nothin'.'

'No,' jeered the woman, 'charity wouldn't have half that lot!'

'Well, why do you want that coat then?' Tommy wanted to know.

'Because my 'usband's just started workin' on the bins, you see, and that'd just do 'im a turn.'

Tommy was even more indignant; his father had only recently stopped wearing the coat. 'It's not for sale no more,' he snapped and stalked into the 'office'. In a low voice he said to Nessy, 'You can go out and sell it to the old faggot if you like.' Nessy swung rhythmically up to the stall, hitching up his pants around his thin waist. 'What was it, lady?' he said.

'That coat. I want it for twenty-five pence.'

'Well, who's arguing with yer, Missus?' He wrapped it up. 'Sold to the lady in the big yeller 'at,' he said.

The crowd giggled. The laughter brought more women over to the stall, and the gang was kept quite busy wrapping up goods. They even ran out of newspaper.

The tragedy struck. A panda car drew up at the kerb and a tall policeman stepped out. At the sight of the uniform the gang stiffened.

'Oh, it's only Constable Jackson', said Tommy.

Constable Jackson strode slowly round the stall and scrutinized the wares. Nessy disappeared into the office; Chai and Raff rearranged a few things which didn't need rearranging, and Tommy stood and waited for whatever was coming.

'Got a licence, have you?' asked Constable Jackson at last.

'A what?' asked Tommy.

'A street traders' licence; have you got one?' repeated the constable patiently.

'What's that?' Tommy asked.

'Ah well, now, it's a bit difficult to explain. It's just a piece of paper, really, with writing on. Gives one permission to sell in the street.'

7

Tommy knew that Constable Jackson knew that he hadn't got one, but he said, 'We'll get one then.'

'Sorry, lad, but you're under age.'

'Well, what can we do?' asked Tommy.

'You can close shop and go home. That's all, I'm afraid.'

Constable Jackson was really very fond of the boys. They never gave him any real trouble. Their idea about the stall was really a very good one and, he thought secretly, the law was often pretty mean.

'Come on,' he said kindly, 'put all that clobber into the back of my car and I'll give you a ride home.'

It was November the fifth. Tommy was glum and silent at breakfast. Then his father said, 'There's going to be a huge firework display in the park tonight. Why don't you go there, Tommy?' He knew what his son was fretting about.

'The park!' exclaimed Tommy. 'The park! We wanted it in our own street, same as usual.'

'Now listen, our Tommy, every year some poor kids get burnt up. Nobody thinks it's going to be them. But every kid what gets burnt belongs to *somebody*. That's why the Corpy are putting on their own display. I bet they spends a hundred pounds on *their* fireworks.'

'More like two hundred, Dad,' put in Mrs Mac, 'and it all comes out of our rates, so you go to it, love.'

Tommy thought about this on the way to school. A hundred, or two hundred pounds worth of fireworks! It ought to be jolly good. He went about persuading Raff, Chai and Nessy that it was a cunning idea to go to the park.

As bad luck would have it Mr Jones decided to have an assembly. And as bad luck would have it twice in the same five minutes, Tommy found himself sitting next to Casey.

'Where're you having yours?' Casey hissed.

'Our what?' asked Tommy, acting as dumb as possible.

'Your bonfire.'

'Bonfire did you say? We aren't bothering this year. Going to the park we are.'

'The park!' hooted Casey. 'With all that lot of posh cissies from Childwell? Oh diddums!'

'Well, we just ain't wastin' our money when we can go and see the Corpy's fireworks for free,' said Tommy. 'It's daft to waste money.' Inwardly he was seething, and longing to crush Casey's toes under his boot.

That evening, Mrs Mac got the tea ready early; then she put an extra vest on Charlie.

'Are you coming too?' she asked Maureen and Stevey.

'You must be joking!' laughed Stevey.

Maureen didn't think the question needed an answer so she didn't trouble to give one.

'You're not coming with us, Mam, are you?' asked Tommy in consternation.

'Of course I am,' replied Mrs Mac. 'It's dark in that park. And anyway, I want to walk some of the fat off me. Also, you might go and lose our Charlie.'

In a way, Tommy didn't really mind his mother coming, just so long as Casey didn't notice.

'Mam, we'll meet you at the corner,' he said.

'Alright,' said Mrs Mac, 'I've got some stuff to buy anyway.'

As luck would have it for a change, all that Casey saw was Tommy and his gang sloping up the street.

The park was almost pitch dark. Tommy had to admit that it really was quite exciting. In the distance, car lights moved without ceasing. But the trees nearby were dark and ghostly.

'Now you hold on tight, Charlie,' warned Mrs Mac. Her breath was like smoke, and Tommy Mac felt strangely comforted by the presence of her round homely figure. Raff, Chai and Nessy seemed to have the same feeling. They chattered excitedly and ran figure-eights in the black wet grass.

'Give over!' cried Mrs Mac happily.

Against the light of a massive bonfire the boys could make out a crowd of hundreds of people.

'Hey look!' cried Mrs Mac. 'Isn't that the mayor?'

'Dunno, is it?' Tommy wasn't interested in the mayor.

'Yes, I'm sure it is. And there's Councillor Bush over there, sitting next to Lady . . .'

She was interrupted by a sudden flash of catherine-wheels.

9

They blazed out the word 'Welcome' and were followed by a burst of applause.

'Gosh!' gasped Tommy.

'Gosh!' said the gang.

'I want to go home!' wailed Charlie, terrified.

'It's alright, love,' comforted Mrs Mac. 'Come under my coat.'

Peering through the buttonhole of his mother's large coat, Charlie watched the next burst of fireworks. A dozen rockets zipped into the sky and burst into a cluster of fairy-like green and orange stars.

'Gosh!' whistled Tommy and his friends once again.

'Tee hee hee!' wheezed Charlie, coming out into the open, no longer scared.

There seemed to be no pause between one lot of fireworks and the next. The gang soon grew tired of saying 'gosh'.

'I ain't never going to buy them from a shop again,' vowed Chai.

'My dad was right, wasn't he!' crowed Tommy.

'Yes, and don't forget we've still got all that money from the stall,' Raff reminded him.

'So we have,' said Tommy absently, as at least twenty Roman candles turned the darkness bright pink.

Meanwhile, back in Paradise Way, a huge bonfire was crackling. It belonged to Casey, Akim and Dyson. There were not many fireworks, just an odd bang here and there, but the flames were fifteen feet high. Doors began to open and angry women and their husbands peered out.

'Get that thing out!' they shouted. 'It's too big, you little hooligans!'

'You'll be cracking our windows,' complained Mr Mac.

In reply, Casey, Akim and Dyson lit sparklers and whooped round their fire like Red Indians. Other children, who had long ago spent their 'Guy' money on sweets, whooped after them. Count and Dracula, shut up in the back yard, howled like a couple of coyotes in pain.

Minutes later a fire engine appeared. Someone had evidently phoned for it.

'Alright, clear off!' shouted the firemen.

They fixed up their hoses, ignoring the rage of the children, the impolite criticism, and the odd lump of wood that came flying their way, and they squirted Casey's bonfire out of existence. 'And I should think so!' snorted the Paradise Way grown-ups. 'Little hooligans!'

At ten o'clock – as late as that – Mrs Mac and her brood came joyfully down the street. They were eating fish and chips.

'What's this, then?' asked Mrs Mac. 'All this mess here?'

A sodden black mass blocked the centre of the road.

'Bet I know what it is!' exploded Tommy; 'it's Casey's bonfire.'

'Oh, I bet it is!' cried the others, falling about in ecstasy.

'Ah, poor kids,' sympathized Mrs Mac kindly. 'You are a mean lot.'

'Well, Mam, Casey's so big-headed,' defended Tommy.

'And you're not?' she asked. 'Come on, villain,' she laughed, giving Tommy a friendly thump around the head.

'See you tomorrow,' Tommy called after his friends.

What the Neighbours Did

PHILIPPA PEARCE

Mum didn't like the neighbours, although – as we were the end cottage of the row – we only had one, really: Dirty Dick. Beyond him, the Macys.

Dick lived by himself – they said there used to be a wife, but she'd run away years ago; so now he lived as he wanted, which Mum said was like a pig in a pig-sty. Once I told Mum that I envied him, and she blew me up for it. Anyway, I'd have liked some of the things he had. He had two cars, although not for driving. He kept rabbits in one, and hens roosted in the other. He sold the eggs, which made part of his living. He made the rest from dealing in old junk (and in the village they said that he'd a stocking full of gold sovereigns which he kept under the mattress of his bed). Mostly he went about on foot, with his handcart for the junk; but he also rode a tricycle. The boys used to jeer at him sometimes, and once I asked him why he didn't ride a bicycle like everyone else. He said he liked a tricycle because you could go as slowly as you wanted, looking at things properly, without ever falling off.

Mrs Macy didn't like Dirty Dick any more than my Mum did, but then she disliked everybody anyway. She didn't like Mr Macy. He was retired, and every morning in all weathers Mrs Macy'd turn him out into the garden and lock the door against him and make him stay there until he'd done as much work as she thought right. She'd put his dinner out to him through the scullery window. She couldn't bear to have anything alive about the place (you couldn't count old Macy himself, Dad used to say). That was one of the reasons why she didn't think much of us, with our dog and cat and Nora's two love-birds in a cage. Dirty Dick's hens and rabbits were even worse, of course.

Then the affair of the yellow dog made the Macys really hate

13

Dirty Dick. It seems that old Mr Macy secretly got himself a dog. He never had any money of his own, because his wife made him hand it over, every week; so Dad reckoned that he must have begged the dog off someone who'd otherwise have had it destroyed.

The dog began as a secret, which sounds just about impossible, with Mrs Macy around. But every day Mr Macy used to take his dinner and eat it in his tool-shed, which opened on the side furthest from the house. That must have been his temptation; but none of us knew he'd fallen into it, until one summer evening we heard a most awful screeching from the Macys' house.

'That's old Ma Macy screaming,' said Dad, spreading his bread and butter.

'Oh, dear!' said Mum, jumping up and then sitting down again. 'Poor old Mr Macy!' But Mum was afraid of Mrs Macy. 'Run upstairs, boy, and see if you can see what's going on.'

So I did. I was just in time for the excitement, for, as I leaned out of the window, the Macys' back door flew open. Mr Macy came out first, with his head down and his arms sort of curved above it; and Mrs Macy came out close behind him, aiming at his head with a light broom – but aiming quite hard. She was screeching words, although it was difficult to pick out any of them. But some words came again and again, and I began to follow: Mr Macy had brought hairs with him into the house – short, curly, yellowish hairs, and he'd left those hairs all over the upholstery, and they must have come from a cat or a dog or a hamster or I don't know what, and so on and so on. Whatever the creature was, he'd been keeping it in the tool-shed, and turn it out he was going to, this very minute.

As usual, Mrs Macy was right about what Mr Macy was going to do.

He opened the shed-door and out ambled a dog – a big, yellowy-white old dog, looking a bit like a sheep, somehow, and about as quick-witted. As though it didn't notice what a tantrum Mrs Macy was in, it blundered gently towards her, and she lifted her broom high, and Mr Macy covered his eyes; and then Mrs Macy let out a real scream – a plain shriek – and dropped the broom and shot indoors and slammed the door after her.

The dog seemed puzzled, naturally; and so was I. It lumbered around towards Mr Macy, and then I saw its head properly, and that it had the most extraordinary eyes – like headlamps, somehow. I don't mean as big as headlamps, of course, but with a kind of whitish glare to them. Then I realized that the poor old thing must be blind.

The dog had raised its nose inquiringly towards Mr Macy, and Mr Macy had taken one timid, hopeful step towards the dog, when one of the sash-windows of the house went up and Mrs Macy leaned out. She'd recovered from her panic, and she gave Mr Macy his orders. He was to take that disgusting animal and turn it out into the road, where he must have found it in the first place.

I knew that old Macy would be too dead scared to do anything else but what his wife told him.

I went down again to where the others were having tea.

'Well?' said Mum.

I told them, and I told them what Mrs Macy was making Mr Macy do to the blind dog. 'And if it's turned out like that on the road, it'll be killed by the first car that comes along.'

There was a pause, when even Nora seemed to be thinking; but I could see from their faces what they were thinking.

Dad said at last: 'That's bad. But we've four people in this little house, and a dog already, and a cat and two birds. There's no room for anything else.'

'But it'll be killed.'

'No,' said Dad. 'Not if you go at once, before any car comes, and take that dog down to the village, to the police station. Tell them it's a stray.'

'But what'll they do with it?'

Dad looked as though he wished I hadn't asked that, but he said: 'Nothing, I expect. Well, they might hand it over to the Cruelty to Animals people.'

'And what'll *they* do with it?'

Dad was rattled. 'They do what they think best for animals – I should have thought they'd have taught you that at school.

15

For goodness' sake, boy!'

Dad wasn't going to say any more, nor Mum, who'd been listening with her lips pursed up. But everyone knew that the most likely thing was that an old, blind, ownerless dog would be destroyed.

But anything would be better than being run over and killed by a car just as you were sauntering along in the evening sunlight; so I started out of the house after the dog.

There he was, sauntering along, just as I'd imagined him. No sign of Mr Macy, of course: he'd have been called back indoors by his wife.

As I ran to catch up with the dog, I saw Dirty Dick coming home, and nearer the dog than I was. He was pushing his handcart, loaded with the usual bits of wood and other junk. He saw the dog coming and stopped, and waited; the dog came on hesitantly towards him.

'I'm coming for him,' I called.

'Ah,' said Dirty Dick. 'Yours?' He held out his hand towards the dog – the hand that my mother always said she could only bear to take hold of if the owner had to be pulled from certain death in a quicksand. Anyway, the dog couldn't see the colour of it, and it positively seemed to like the smell; it came on.

'No,' I said. 'Macys were keeping it, but Mrs Macy turned it out. I'm going to take it down to the police as a stray. What do you think they'll do with it?'

Dirty Dick never said much; this time he didn't answer. He just bent down to get his arm round the dog and in a second he'd hoisted him up on top of all the stuff in the cart. Then he picked up the handles and started off again.

So the Macys saw the blind dog come back to the row of cottages in state, as you might say, sitting on top of half a broken lavatory-seat on the very pinnacle of Dirty Dick's latest load of junk.

Dirty Dick took good care of his animals, and he took good care of this dog he adopted. It always looked well-fed and well-brushed. Sometimes he'd take it out with him, on the end of a long string; mostly he'd leave it comfortably at home. When it lay out in the back garden, old Mr Macy used to look at it longingly over the fence. Once or twice I saw him poke his fingers through, towards what had once been *his* dog. But that had been for only a very short, dark time in the shed; and the old dog never moved towards the fingers. Then 'Macy!' his terrible old wife would call from the house, and he'd have to go.

Then suddenly we heard that Dirty Dick had been robbed – old Macy came round specially to tell us. 'An old sock stuffed with pound notes, that he kept up the bedroom chimney. Gone. Hasn't he *told* you?'

'No,' said Mum, 'but we don't have a lot to do with him.' She might have added that we didn't have a lot to do with the Macys either – I think this was the first time I'd ever seen one step over our threshold in a neighbourly way.

'You're thick with him sometimes,' said old Macy, turning on me. 'Hasn't he told *you* all about it?'

'Me?' I said. 'No.'

'Mind you, the whole thing's not to be wondered at,' said the old man. 'Front and back doors never locked, and money kept in the house. That's a terrible temptation to anyone with a weakness that way. A temptation that shouldn't have been put.'

'I daresay,' said Mum. 'It's a shame, all the same. His savings.'

'Perhaps the police'll be able to get it back for him,' I said. 'There'll be clues.'

The old man jumped – a nervous sort of jump. 'Clues? You think the police will find clues? I never thought of that. No, I did not. But has he gone to the police, anyway, I wonder. That's what I wonder. That's what I'm asking you.' He paused, and I realized that he meant me again. 'You're thick with him, boy. Has he gone to the police? That's what I want to know . . .'

His mouth seemed to have filled with saliva, so that he had to stop to swallow, and couldn't say more. He was in a state, all right.

At that moment Dad walked in from work and wasn't best pleased to find that visitor instead of his tea waiting; and Mr Macy went.

Dad listened to the story over tea, and across the fence that evening he spoke to Dirty Dick and said he was sorry to hear about the money.

'Who told you?' asked Dirty Dick.

Dad said that old Macy had told us. Dirty Dick just nodded; he didn't seem interested in talking about it any more. Over that week-end no police came to the row, and you might have thought that old Macy had invented the whole thing, except that Dirty Dick had not contradicted him.

On Monday I was rushing off to school when I saw Mr Macy in their front garden, standing just between a big laurel bush and the fence. He looked straight at me and said 'Good morning' in a kind of whisper. I don't know which was odder – the whisper, or his wishing me good morning. I answered in rather a shout, because I was late and hurrying past. His mouth had opened as though he meant to say more, but then it shut, as though he'd changed his mind. That was all, that morning.

The next morning he was in just the same spot again, and hailed me in the same way; and this time I was early, so I stopped.

He was looking shiftily about him, as though someone might be spying on us; but at least his wife couldn't be doing that, because the laurel bush was between him and their front windows. There was a tiny pile of yellow froth at one corner of his mouth, as though he'd been chewing his words over in advance. The sight of the froth made me want not to stay; but then the way he looked at me made me feel that I had to. No, it just made me; I had to.

'Look what's turned up in our back garden,' he said, in the same whispering voice. And he held up a sock so dirty – partly with soot – and so smelly that it could only have been Dirty Dick's. It was stuffed full of something – pound notes, in fact. Old Macy's story of the robbery had been true in every detail.

I gasped at him.

'It's all to go back,' said Mr Macy. 'Back exactly to where it came from.' And then, as though I'd suggested the obvious – that he should hand the sock back to Dirty Dick himself with the same explanation just given to me: 'No, no. It must go back as though it had never been – never been taken away.' He couldn't use the word 'stolen'. 'Mustn't have the police poking round us. Mrs Macy wouldn't like it.' His face twitched at his own mention of her; he leaned forward. 'You must put it back, boy. Put it back for me and keep your mouth shut. Go on. Yes.'

He must have been half out of his mind to think that I should do it, especially as I still didn't twig why. But as I stared at his twitching face I suddenly did understand. I mean, that old Macy had taken the sock, out of spite, and then lost his nerve.

He must have been half out of his mind to think that I would do that for him; and yet I did it. I took the sock and put it inside my jacket and turned back to Dirty Dick's cottage. I walked boldly up to the front door and knocked, and of course there was no answer. I knew he was already out with the cart.

There wasn't a sign of anyone looking, either from our house or the Macys'. (Mr Macy had already disappeared.) I tried the door and it opened, as I knew it would. I stepped inside and closed it behind me.

I'd never been inside before. The house was dirty, I suppose, and smelt a bit, but not really badly. It smelt of Dirty Dick and hens and rabbits – although it was untrue that he kept either hens or rabbits indoors, as Mrs Macy said. It smelt of dog, too, of course.

Opening straight off the living-room, where I stood, was the twisty, dark little stairway – exactly as in our cottage next door.

I went up.

The first room upstairs was full of junk. A narrow passage-way had been kept clear to the second room, which opened off the first one. This was Dirty Dick's bedroom, with the bed unmade, as it probably was for weeks on end.

There was the fire-place, too, with a good deal of soot which had recently been brought down from the chimney. You couldn't miss seeing that – Dirty Dick couldn't have missed it, at the time. Yet he'd done nothing about his theft. In fact, I realized now that he'd probably said nothing either. The only person who'd let the cat out of the bag was poor old Macy himself.

I'd been working this out as I looked at the fire-place, standing quite still. Round me the house was silent. The only sound came from outside, where I could see a hen perched on the bumper of the old car in the back garden, clucking for an egg newly laid. But when she stopped, there came another, tiny sound that terrified me: the click of a front gate opening. Feet were clumping up to the front door . . .

I stuffed the sock up the chimney again, any old how, and was out of that bedroom in seconds; but on the threshold of the junk-room I stopped, fixed by the headlamp glare of the old blind dog. He must have been there all the time, lying under a three-legged washstand, on a heap of rags. All the time he would have been watching me, if he'd had his eyesight. He didn't move.

Meanwhile the front door had opened and the footsteps had clumped inside, and stopped. There was a long pause, while I stared at the dog, who stared at me; and down below Dirty Dick listened and waited – he must have heard my movement just before.

At last: 'Well,' he called, 'why don't you come down?'

There was nothing else to do but go. Down that dark, twisty stair, knowing that Dirty Dick was waiting for me at the bottom. He was a big man, and strong. He heaved his junk about like nobody's business.

But when I got down, he wasn't by the foot of the stairs; he was standing by the open door, looking out, with his back to me. He hadn't been surprised to hear someone upstairs in his house, uninvited; but when he turned round from the doorway, I could see that he hadn't expected to see *me*. He'd expected someone else – old Macy, I suppose.

I wanted to explain that I'd only put the sock back – there was soot all over my hands, plain to be seen, of course – and that I'd had nothing to do with taking it in the first place. But he'd drawn his thick brows together as he looked at me, and he jerked his head towards the open door. I was frightened, and I went past him without saying anything. I was late for school now, anyway, and I ran.

I didn't see Dirty Dick again.

Later that morning Mum chose to give him a talking to, over the back fence, about locking his doors against pilferers in future. She says he didn't say he would, he didn't say he wouldn't; and he didn't say anything about anything having been stolen, or returned.

Soon after that, Mum saw him go out with the handcart with all his rabbits in a hutch, and he came back later without them. He did the same with his hens. We heard later that he'd given them away in the village; he hadn't even bothered to try to sell them.

Then he went round to Mum, wheeling the tricycle. He said he'd decided not to use it any more, and I could have it. He didn't leave any message for me.

Later still, Mum saw him set off for the third time that day with his hand cart: not piled very high even, but with the old dog sitting on top. And that was the last that anyone saw of him.

He must have taken very little money with him: they found the sooty sock, still nearly full, by the rent-book on the mantelpiece. There was plenty to pay the rent due and to pay for cleaning up the house and the garden for the next tenant. He must have been fed up with being a householder, Dad said – and with having neighbours. He just wanted to turn tramp, and he did.

It was soon after he'd gone that I said to Mum that I envied him, and she blew me up, and went on and on about soap and water and fecklessness.All the same, I did envy him. I didn't even have the fun with his tricycle that he'd had. I never rode it, although I wanted to, because I was afraid that people I knew would laugh at me.

21

A Bit of Bread and Jam

BILL NAUGHTON

It was one o'clock on Saturday afternoon, and eleven of us boys were setting out from our street to go fishing. Suddenly the woman at the end house, whose name was Mrs Hoskey, bobbed her head out of the door and called out to us.

'Hy, will one of you boys go an errand for me?'

We none of us answered. We all knew her. She was one of those women who liked to have you mugging around for an hour, and would then promise you a penny, which you never got.

'Hy,' she called again after us. 'Don't go,' whispered Felix Stringfellow. 'It's not worth it. She'll send you to the tripe shop for some trotters, to Clarke's for some toffees, to the paper-shop for some love books, an' when you've worn your shoe leather away, she'll give you a miserable bit of bread an' jam.'

'A rotten jam butty,' said Sammy Feathers.

Felix was our gang leader, and we none of us went against him. He had turned fifteen and was already working in the factory.

'Why don't you send Albert?' he called, with a beckon of his thumb at little Mr Hoskey, who was pegging out washing in the back street.

'He's busy,' she said. Then she caught my eye. 'Hy, you, Billy – you'll not see me stuck?'

She was a big fat woman with red hair, and I'd once heard somebody say she could put the evil eye on you. I didn't want that happening when I was going off fishing.

'I'll not be long, lads,' I said.

'Gaa,' snorted Felix, 'a fat lot you'll get.' And off he went with the gang.

He was right about that errand, except that she had a

22

quarter-ounce of snuff as well. And he was dead right about the jam butty.

'There's a nice bit of our Albert's bakin',' she said, wrapping it up in paper and trying to make it look a lot.

'You can't give that to young Billy, Ada,' cried Albert. 'I tell you it didn't rise properly.'

'If you poke your nose into my business,' she said to him, 'I'll put you up the chimney. S'help me.'

Little Albert looked uncomfortable and unhappy. 'But it hasn't risen,' he said. Then he looked at me as though he was going to burst out crying. 'Billy, don't eat it!' At that his wife let out one roar, and I went off with my jam butty.

One bite convinced me that his advice was sound. I chewed it for a hundred yards or so, just to give it a chance. But then I marked one of those wide sewer grids along the street, and I dropped the mouthful down. Then I ran to Pike's lodge.

Every inch of the muddy bank was thronged with kids of all ages, fishing away with all their might. There was a din of argument going on, the constant *perlop* of a worm on a pin hitting the water, and the excited *perluff* of a writhing stickle-back being pulled out. I raced up the bank, kicked up a sod of grass with the toe of my clog, pawed madly into the soil, grabbed a worm, and, unreeling my line at the same time, I hurried off to my own gang.

Felix was up to his shins in mud, and held a line in each hand. Beside him was a great big toffee-tin that was already heaving with fish. Just as I forced my way in beside him he drew in both lines.

'Seven!' I yelled, seeing them wriggling in the sunshine. 'Four red doctors among 'em.'

Instead of slipping them off, Felix looked at them with a sour face, and even stood watching while two got away.

'Have you gone daft?' I said.

'There's nowt to it,' said Felix. 'I'm fed up to the eye tooth.' He looked round at the mob. 'You throw in an' they're on before the worm hits the water. It aren't fishin' – it's mass suicide. Even wenches are catchin' 'em.' Then he picked up the can in both hands and flung all the fish back in.

23

We could hardly believe our own eyes. Not that I felt so bad, because I hadn't caught any. 'There's nowt to it,' said Felix.

'What's on your mind?' said Sammy Feathers.

'I want to do summat as needs a bit of doin',' said Felix. 'Such as catching a carp. A carp aren't like a stickleback – it don't bite.'

'What does it do?' I said.

'*Sucks*,' said Felix. 'A carp gives a suck at the bait to see if it likes it. The float does no more than tremble. Then tha strikes. That's what I call fishin'.'

'But where can we catch carp, Felix?'

'Our mill lodge.'

'Pratt an' Dyson's?' said Sammy. 'Not a chance!'

'Why? The watchman?'

'No, the *carp*. Our old chap has fished every lodge, lake, an' canal in the British Isles, an' he reckons there's no fish in this wide world wants as much catching as one of Pratt an' Dyson's carp. They're that pampered that they don't even suck.'

'What do they do?'

'*Sniff*. They just sniff the bait – an' you gotta strike then.'

'That sort of fishing,' said Felix, 'I'd say there was summat to.'

'Aye, but nobody ever catches any.'

'You don't have to tell me,' said Felix. 'I work there. Come on, chaps.'

We all followed him to the back of Pratt and Dyson's mill. A very high fence with a barbed-wire top surrounded the mill lodge. 'The watchman has his tea from four to half-past,' said Felix. 'He's as deaf as a doornail an' can't see a yard in front of him, so don't worry.'

I saw a knot-hole in the wood and I peeped through. 'No use, there's one chap fishing.'

Felix shoved me out of the way and had a look for himself. 'It's our managing director,' he said. 'Charlie Pratt. Come on, give me a cock up, an' I'll see what he says.' We gave him a leg up, and he got his head over the top. ''Llo, Mister Pratt! I work in number seven room under Alec Ackers. Would it be

25

all right if me an' my mates had a quiet ten minutes with you?'

'It will be quiet,' we heard him say. 'I've been here since early morning an' never had a stir. But if you can get in, you're welcome to it. Don't say I gave you permission.'

'Okay, lads,' said Felix, 'he says we can go in.' Then he hurried along the boards, tapping each one. 'There's a false 'un, if I can find it. Ah, here it is.' A slat of wood gave way, and Felix crept in, we all followed, and he replaced it. For a minute none of us spoke. It was as though we had entered some wonderful land, after all the din and mud of the Pike lodge. Here it was beautifully quiet, everything spotless; the water was pale green, and the fat, lazy carp, some a lovely red and gold, were gliding about in the depths.

We began to feel about in our pockets for hooks and catgut. 'Oh, but what about bait?' exclaimed Sammy Feathers.

'Crikey, these won't look at worms,' said Felix. 'We need some good dough.'

'You can divide this bit up, lads,' said Mr Pratt. 'I've just had about enough.'

There was a rush for the ball of bait. Before I could get there it was all gone. 'Hy, what about me?' I said.

'*Sh, sh,*' whispered Felix, 'I hope we're not driving you away, Mister Pratt?'

'Ten hours, laddie,' he said, 'without a bite, is enough even for me.' He began to pack up his fishing gear slowly.

In no time they all had their lines on the go. And there I was without a crumb of bait for mine. I went mooching away to a corner to sulk. Then suddenly, I felt the remnant of the jam butty in my pocket. I turned away from the others, got it out and, unable to separate the bread from the jam, I put the lot in my hanky, kneaded it up, adding drops of spittle to make it doughy. I took a peck between finger and thumb, rolled it into a pellet, carefully pressed it on to my hook, made myself comfortable, looked at the water, then softly cast in.

Suddenly my float disappeared. What's up? I thought, what's up? Where's it gone? I half pulled out, felt something there, and struck. Up came my line out of the water. Wriggling and twittering at the end of it was a lovely fat carp!

Flummoxed for a second or so, I could no more than stare at it and think: Is this happening to me? And then I heard Felix give a shout, 'Quick, som'dy, where's can?' I turned and saw them all staring open-gobbed at me. I swung the line in, and by luck my left hand grasped the fish first time. It felt as thick as a fat polony sausage and full of life. Some power came to my fingers and extricated the hook. With my left hand I held the fish under water, not even bothering to look down at it, and as Felix spluttered to get the can filled with water I remarked casually, 'What's all the fuss about, man? Tak' your time.'

I rolled another pellet of bait, while a cluster of heads was over the tin. As I cast in again, heard the pleasant *ping* of the tiny weights striking the water surface, I felt a relaxed calm coming to me. Then I gave a jump as there was a cry from Felix: 'You're under!'

I gave a jerk. The gleam of a carp in the air, jiggling the next instant on the bank. I just blurted out, 'Tak' it off, Felix.' Eagerly he obeyed. I kept my face down. It didn't feel like it belonged to me. But I had wits enough to stick the hanky of bait down in my pocket. Little Albert's baking, I thought, worth a fortune.

In no time they had crowded my pitch. Not a single bite, however, but mine. I missed three, and moved farther along the bank. Mr Pratt gave me a begging look, and I slipped him a morsel of bait. He landed two beauties in about five minutes. As for me, I was catching them and missing them every other minute.

'*Sniff?*' remarked Felix to Sammy. 'They're biting like tiger sharks, tell your father. Hy, we've just a round dozen – what about getting another can?'

But the watchman arrived just then. 'You might be the boss during the week,' he said to Mr Pratt, 'but I'm in charge over the week-end. I'm not having it.'

I was glad to get away, for the strain was telling.

'You can all have one apiece,' I said, feeling generous, 'an' I'll have two.' The secret of the bait I didn't share, even turning down a hint of a bribe from Mr Pratt. With carp fetching fourpence each, and gold ones a tanner, I reckoned

I'd make a fortune over the season. All I had to do was play my cards right with little Albert and the watchman.

'I say chaps,' said Felix, as we turned the street corner, 'what's everybody out for? What are they all chunnering about? Look, Bill, the ambulance outside your door.'

At that moment Felix's mother spotted me and let out a yell: 'He's here! He's here!'

Out came my mother, running to me, with a policeman beside her. 'Are you all right, love?' she screamed, putting her arms round me.

I shoved her off. 'Let go! 'Course I am.'

Then the policeman calmed her down. 'He'll be all right, Ma.' He turned to me. 'Are you the lad that had the jam butty given you by Mrs Hoskey at the end house at half-past one to-day?'

'Aye, I am.'

'How do you feel?'

'Champion. Leastways, I did.'

'Come on, laddie,' he said, patting me on the head, 'in the ambulance.'

'What for? Like this?'

'Aye, there's no time to dress up. Keep calm, Ma,' he said, helping my mother in.

'What's up, Mum?' I heard Felix ask.

'Little Albert,' she said, 'bashed Ada on the napper with a mallet.'

'About time somebody did.'

'Only stunned her.'

'What a pity!'

'That's why he gave himself up – to get safely out of her way.'

The driver shut the white ambulance door.

'When did you eat it, sonny?' asked the attendant as we moved off.

'Eat what?'

'The jam butty.'

They were gazing at me pitifully, and my mother was crying her eyes out.

'I didn't.'

28

'What?' yelled the attendant, rapping on the panel. 'Stop!'

'What did you do with it?' asked the policeman.

I thought for a minute before answering. I pictured all the carp I was going to catch. 'The first grid I came to,' I said, 'I put it down.'

'Oh, I'll warm you, my lad,' cried my mother, grabbing me by the shoulders, 'for givin' us all such a fright.'

'You'll be all right now, Ma,' the policeman opened the door and let her out. 'I'll have him home with you in ten minutes.' Then he turned to the attendant. 'Drop us off at the town-hall – our inspector wants a word with the lad.'

Into the police-inspector's office I went, and all my words were taken down in writing.

'Tell the prisoner to stop worrying about the lad,' said the inspector to a jailer. 'Tell him he never ate it.'

As the policeman was taking me back to the tram I said to him: 'What's all this fuss about a jam butty?'

'It were *dosed*,' he stooped and whispered in my ear, 'dosed heavy.'

'Whatever with?'

'*Arsenic!*'

For a moment I had to put my hand against the wall just to steady my knees.

'Enough,' went on the policeman, 'to kill a regiment. It were all the top off the jam – where he'd planted it for her. An' the bread itself were fair weighted wi' it. Don't breathe a word, lad, but it's God's mercy you're not stretched stone stiff in the morgue this very minute.'

When I reached the street corner I was suddenly confronted by Felix.

'Hy, know what? Know what, Bill?' he cried in alarm, 'the fish, every bloomin' one swimmin' round like mad, swellin' up, an' dropping stone stiff dead!'

Seeing him so upset over a few paltry carp caused a strange calm to come over me. 'Felix,' I said, putting a hand on his shoulder, 'forget it. There's nowt to it.'

Leaving him staring flabbergasted at me, I staggered lightly up the street, neither knowing nor caring whether they'd fuss me at home or give me a right good hiding.

The Apple of Trouble

JOAN AIKEN

It was a black day for the Armitage family when Great-Uncle
Gavin retired. In fact, as Mark pointed out, Uncle Gavin did
not exactly retire; he was pushed. He had been High Commissioner of Mbutam-Mbutaland, which had suddenly decided it
needed a High Commissioner no longer, but would instead
become the Republic of Mbutambuta. So Sir Gavin Armitage,
K.C.M.G., O.B.E., D.S.O., and so forth, was suddenly turned
loose on the world, and because he had expected to continue
living at the High Commissioner's Residence for years to come
and had no home of his own, he moved in with the parents of
Mark and Harriet.

The first disadvantage was that he had to sleep in the ghost's
room. Mr Peake was nice about it, he said he quite understood,
and they would probably shake down together very well, he
had been used to all sorts of odd company in his three hundred
years. But after a few weeks of Great-Uncle Gavin's keep-fit
exercises, coughing, thumping, harrumphing, snoring, and
blazing open windows, Mr Peake became quite thin and pale
(for a ghost); he migrated through the wall into the room next
door, explaining apologetically that he wasn't getting a wink of
sleep. Unfortunately the room next door was a bathroom, and
Mr Armitage complained that it gave him the jumps to see a
ghostly face suddenly loom up beside his in the mirror when
he was shaving. Great-Uncle Gavin never noticed Mr Peake at
all. He was not sensitive. Besides he had other things to think
about.

One of his main topics of conversation was how disgracefully
the children had been brought up. He was horrified at the way
they were allowed to live all over the house, instead of being
pent in some upstairs nursery.

'Little gels should be seen and not heard,' he boomed at

30

Harriet whenever she opened her mouth. To get her out from underfoot during the holidays he insisted on her enrolling in a domestic science course run by a Professor Grimalkin who had recently come to live in the village.

As for Mark, he had hardly a minute's peace.

'God bless my soul, boy' – nearly all Great-Uncle Gavin's remarks began with this request – 'God bless my soul, what are you doing now? *Reading?* God bless my soul, do you want to grow up a muff?'

'A muff, Great-Uncle? What is a muff, exactly?' And Mark pulled out the notebook in which he was keeping a glossary of Great-Uncle Gavin.

'A muff, why, a muff is a – a funk, sir, a duffer, a frowst, a tug, a swot, a miserable little sneaking *milksop!*'

Mark was so busy writing down all these words that he forgot to be annoyed.

'You ought to be out of doors, sir, ought to be out playin' footer.'

'But you need twenty-two people for that,' Mark pointed out, 'and there's only Harriet and me. Besides, it's summer. And Harriet is a bit of a duffer at French cricket.'

'Don't be impudent, boy! Gad, when I was your age I'd have been out collectin' birds' eggs.'

'*Birds' eggs!*' said Mark, scandalized. 'But I'm a subscribing member of the Royal Society for the Protection of Birds.'

'Butterflies, then,' growled his Great-Uncle.

'I read a book, Great-Uncle, that said all the butterflies were being killed by indiscriminate use of pesticides and what's left ought to be carefully preserved.'

Sir Gavin was turning egg-plant colour and seemed likely to explode.

'Boy's a regular sea-lawyer,' he said furiously. 'Grow up into one of those confounded trade-union johnnies. Why don't you go out on your velocipede, then, sir? At your age I was as keen as mustard, by gad; used to ride miles on my penny-farthing, rain or shine.'

'No bike,' said Mark. 'Only the unicorn, and he's got a swelled fetlock; we're fomenting it.'

31

'Unicorn! Never heard such namby-pamby balderdash in my life! Here,' Great-Uncle Gavin said, 'what's your weekly allowance when your pater's at home?'

With the disturbed family ghost and the prospect of Uncle Gavin's indefinite stay to depress them, Mr and Mrs Armitage had rather meanly decided that they were in need of three weeks in Madeira, and had left the day before.

'Half a crown a week,' said Mark. 'I've had three weeks in advance.'

'How much does a bike cost nowadays?'

'Oh, I daresay you could pick one up for thirty-five pounds.'

'*What?*' Great-Uncle Gavin nearly fell out of his chair but then, rallying, he pulled seven five-pound notes out of his ample wallet. 'Here, then, boy; this is an advance on your allowance for the next two hundred and eighty weeks. I'll collect it from your governor when he comes home. Cut along, now, and buy a bicycle, an' go for a topping spin and *don't let me see your face again until supper-time.*'

'But I don't want a bicycle,' Mark said.

'Be off, boy, make yourself scarce, don't argue! – On second thoughts, 'spose I'd better come with you, to make sure you don't spend the money on some appallin' book about nature.'

So Great-Uncle Gavin stood over Mark while the latter unwillingly and furiously purchased a super-excellent low-slung bicycle with independent suspension, disc brakes, three-inch tyres, five-speed, and an outboard motor. None of which assets did Mark want in the least, as who would when they had a perfectly good unicorn to ride?

'Now, be off with you and see how quickly you can get to Brighton and back.'

Day after day thereafter, no sooner had breakfast been eaten than Mark was hounded from the house by his relentless Great-Uncle and urged to try and better his yesterday's time to Brighton.

'Gosh, he must have led those Mbutam-Mbutas a life,' he muttered darkly in the privacy of Harriet's room.

'I suppose he's old and we ought to be patient with him,' Harriet said. She was pounding herbs in a mortar for her domestic science homework.

The trouble was, concluded Mark, gloomily pedalling along one afternoon through a heavy summer downpour, that during his forty years among the simple savages Great-Uncle Gavin had acquired the habit of command; it was almost impossible not to obey his orders.

Almost impossible; not quite. Presently the rain increased to a cloudburst.

'Drat Great-Uncle Gavin! I'm not going all the way to Brighton in this,' Mark decided. 'Anyway, why *should* I go to Brighton?'

And he climbed a stile and dashed up a short grassy path to a small near-by church which had a convenient and dry-looking porch. He left his bike on the other side of the stile, for that is another disadvantage of bikes; you can never take them all the way to where you want to go.

The church proved to be chilly and not very interesting, so Mark, who always carried a paperback in his pocket, settled on the porch bench to read until the rain abated. After a while, hearing footsteps, he looked up and saw that a smallish, darkish, foreign-looking man had joined him.

'Nasty afternoon,' Mark said civilly.

'Eh? Yes! Yes indeed.' The man seemed nervous; he kept glancing over his shoulder down the path.

'Is your bicycle, boy, by wall yonder?' he asked by and by.

'Yes it is.'

'Is a fine one,' the man said. 'Very fine one. Would go lickety-spit fast, I daresay?'

'An average of twenty m.p.h.,' Mark said gloomily.

'Will it? Will it so?'

The little man fell silent, glancing out uneasily once more at the rainy dusk, while Mark strained his eyes to see the print of his book. He noticed that his companion seemed to be shuffling about, taking a pack off his back and rummaging among the contents; presently Mark realized that something was being held out to him. He looked up from the page and saw a golden apple – quite a large one, about the size of a Bramley. On one side the gold had a reddish bloom, as if the sun had ripened it.

33

The other side was paler. Somebody had taken two bites out of the red side; Mark wondered what it had done to their teeth. Near the stalk was a dark-brown stain, like a patch of rust.

'Nice, eh?' the little man said, giving the apple to Mark, who nearly dropped it on the flagged floor. It must have weighed at least four pounds.

'Is it real gold all through?' he asked. 'Must be quite valuable.'

'Valuable?' the little man said impressively. 'Such apple is beyond price. You of course well-educated, familiar with Old Testament tale of Adam and Eve?'

'W-why yes,' Mark said, stammering a little. 'But you – you don't mean to say *that* apple –?'

'Self-same one,' the little man said, nodding his head. 'Original bite marks of Adam and Eve before apple carried out of Eden. Then – see stain? Blood of Abel. Cain killed him for apple. Stain will never wash off.'

'Goodness,' Mark said.

'Not all, however – not all at all! Apple of discord – golden apple same which began Trojan War – have heard of such?'

'Why, yes. But – but you're not telling me –'

'Identical apple,' the little man said proudly. 'Apples of Asgard, too? Heard of? Scandinavian golden apples of perpetual youth, guarded by Idhuun?'

'Yes, but you don't –'

'Such was one of those. Not to mention Apples of Hesperides, stolen by Hercules.'

'Hold on – surely it couldn't have been both?'

'Could,' the little man said. 'Was. William Tell's apple – familiar story? – same apple. Newton – apple fell on head, letting in dangerous principle of gravity. This. Atalanta – apple thrown by Milanion to stop her winning race. Also, Prince Ahmed's apple –'

'Stop, stop!' said Mark. 'I don't understand how it could possibly be *all* those.'

But somehow, as he held the heavy, shining thing in his hand, he did believe the little man's story. There was a peculiar, rather nasty fascination about the apple. It scared him, and yet

34

he wanted it.

'So, see,' the little man said, nodding more than ever, 'worth millions pounds. No lie – millions. And yet I give to you –'

'Now, wait a minute –'

'Give in exchange for bicycle, yes? Okay?'

'Well, but – but *why*? Why don't you want the apple?'

'Want bicycle more.' He glanced down the road again, and now Mark guessed.

'Someone's after you – the police? You stole the apple?'

'Not stole, no, no, no! Did swap, like with bicycle, you agree, yes?'

He was already halfway down the path. Hypnotized, Mark watched him climb the stile and mount the bike, wobbling. Suddenly Mark found his voice and called,

'What did you swap for it?'

'Drink of water – in desert, see?'

'Who's chasing you, then?'

By now the little man was chugging down the road and his last word, indistinct, floated back through the rain, something ending in '-ese'; it might have been Greek for all Mark could make of it.

He put the apple in his pocket, which sagged under the weight, and, since the shower was slackening, walked to the road to flag a lift home in the next lorry.

Great-Uncle Gavin nearly burst a blood-vessel when he learned that Mark had exchanged his new bicycle for an apple, albeit a gold one.

'Did what – merciful Providence – an *apple*? – Hesperides? Eden? Asgard? Never heard such a pack of moonshine in all me born – let's see it then. Where is it?'

Mark produced the apple and a curious gleam lit up Uncle Gavin's eye.

'Mind,' he said, 'don't believe a word of the feller's tale, but plain that's val'ble; far too val'ble an article to be in *your* hands, boy. Better give it here at once. I'll get Christie's to value it. And of course we must advertise in *The Times* for the wallah who palmed it off on you – highly illegal transaction, I daresay.'

Mark felt curiously relieved to be rid of the apple, as if a load had been lifted from his mind as well as his pocket.

He ran upstairs whistling. Harriet, as usual, was up in her room mixing things in retorts and crucibles. When Uncle Gavin, as in duty bound, asked each evening what she had been learning that day in her domestic science course, she always replied briefly 'Spelling.' 'Spellin', gel? Rum notion of housekeepin' the johnny seems to have. Still, daresay it keeps you out of mischief.' In fact, as Harriet had confided to Mark, Professor Grimalkin was a retired alchemist who, having failed to find the Philosopher's Stone, was obliged to take in pupils to make ends meet. He was not a very good teacher; his heart wasn't in it. Mark watched Harriet toss a pinch of green powder into a boiling beaker. Half a peach tree shot up, wavered, sagged, and then collapsed. Impatiently Harriet tipped the frothing liquid out of the window and put some more water on to boil.

Then she returned to the window and peered into the dark.

'Funny,' she said. 'There seem to be some people waiting outside the front door. Can't think why they didn't ring the bell. Could you let them in, Mark? My hands are all covered with prussic acid. I expect they're friends of Uncle Gavin's.'

Mark went down and opened the door. Outside, dimly illuminated by the light from the porch, he saw three ladies. They seemed to be dressed in old-fashioned clothes, drainpipe skirts down to their ankles, and cloaks and bonnets rather like those of Salvation Army lasses; their bonnets were perched on thick, lank masses of hair. Mark didn't somehow care for their faces, which resembled those of dogs – but not tame domestic dogs, so much as starved, wild, slightly mad dogs; they stared at Mark hungrily.

'Er – I'm so sorry. Did you ring? Have you been waiting long?' he said.

'A long, long time. Since the world-tree was but a seed in darkness. We are the daughters of Night,' one of them hollowly replied. She moved forward with a leathery rustle.

36

'Oh.' Mark noticed that she had bats' wings. He stepped back a little. 'Do you want to see Great-Uncle – Sir Gavin Armitage? Won't you come in?'

'Nay. We are the watchers by the threshold. Our place is here.'

'Oh, all right. What name shall I say?'

To this question they replied in a sort of gloomy chant, taking it in turns to speak.

'We are the avengers of blood.'

'Sisters of the nymph with the apple-bough, Nemesis.'

'We punish the sin of child against parent –'

'Youth against age –'

'Brother against brother –'

'We are the Erinyes, the Kindly Ones –' (But their expressions were far from kindly, Mark thought.)

'Tisiphone –'

'Alecto –'

'And Megaera.'

'And what did you wish to see Sir Gavin about?' Mark knew his great-uncle hated to be disturbed once he was settled in the evening with a glass of port and *The Times*.

'We attend him who holds the apple.'

'There is blood on it – a brother's blood, shed by a brother.'

'It cries for vengeance.'

'Oh, I *see*!' said Mark, beginning to take in the situation. Now he understood why the little man had been so anxious for a bicycle. 'But, look here, dash it all, Uncle Gavin hasn't shed any blood! That was Cain, and it was a long time ago. I don't see why Uncle should be responsible.'

'He holds the apple.'

'He must bear the guilt.'

'The sins of the fathers are visited on the children.'

'Blood calls for blood.'

Then the three wolfish ladies disconcertingly burst into a sort of hymn, shaking tambourines and beating on them with brass-studded rods which they pulled out from among their draperies:

We are the daughters
Of darkness and time
We follow the guilty
We punish the crime
Nothing but bloodshed
Will settle old scores
So blood has to flow and
That blood must be yours!

When they had finished they fixed their ravenous eyes on
Mark again and the one called Alecto said,

'Where is he?'

Mark felt greatly relieved that Uncle Gavin had taken the
apple away from him and was therefore apparently responsible
for its load of guilt, but as this was a mean thought he tried to
stifle it. Turning (not that he liked having the ladies behind his
back) he went into the sitting-room where Uncle Gavin was
sitting snug by the fire and said,

'There are some callers asking for you, Great-Uncle.'

'God bless my soul, at this time of the evenin'? Who the
deuce –'

Great-Uncle Gavin crossly stumped out to the porch, saying
over his shoulder, 'Why didn't you ask 'em in, boy? Not very
polite to leave 'em standing –'

Then he saw the ladies and his attitude changed. He said
sharply,

'Didn't you see the notice on the gate, my good women? It
says NO HAWKERS OR CIRCULARS. I give handsome
cheques to charity each year at Christmas and make it a rule
never to contribute to door-to-door collections. So be off, if
you please!'

'We do not seek money,' Tisiphone hungrily replied.

'Milk-bottle tops, jumble, old gold, it's all the same. Pack of
meddlesome old maids – I've no time for you!' snapped Sir
Gavin. 'Good night!' And he shut the door smartly in their
faces.

'Have to be firm with that sort of customer,' he told Mark.
'Become a thorough nuisance otherwise – tiresome old harpies.
Got wind of that golden apple, I daresay – shows what happens

when you mix with such people. Shockin' mistake. Take the apple to Christie's tomorrow. Now, please see I'm not disturbed again.' And he returned to the sitting-room.

Mark looked uneasily at the front door but it remained shut; evidently the three Kindly Ones were content to wait outside. But there they stayed; when Mark returned to Harriet's room he looked out of the window and saw them, sombre and immovable, in the shadows outside the porch, evidently prepared to sit out the night.

'Not very nice if they're going to picket our front door from now on,' he remarked gloomily to Harriet. 'Goodness knows what the postman will think. And *I* don't fancy 'em above half. Wonder how we can get rid of them.'

'I've an idea,' Harriet said. 'Professor Grimalkin was talking about them the other day. They are the Furies. But it's awfully hard to shake them off once they're after you.'

'That's gay.'

'There are various things you can do, biting off your finger –'

'Some hope of Uncle Gavin doing that!'

'Or shaving your head.'

'Wouldn't be much use, since he's bald as a bean already.'

'You can bathe seven times in running water or the blood of pigs –'

'He always *does* take a lot of cold baths and we had pork for supper, so plainly that's no go.'

'Well, you can go into exile for a year,' Harriet said.

'I only wish he would.'

'Or build them a grotto, nice and dark, preferably under an ilex tree, and make suitable offerings.'

'Such as what?'

'Anything black, or they rather go for iris flowers. Milk and honey too. And they can be shot with a bow of horn, but that doesn't seem to be very successful as a rule.'

'Oh well, let's try the milk-and-honey and something black for now,' Mark said. 'And I'll make a bow of horn tomorrow – I've got Candleberry's last year's horn in my room somewhere.' Candleberry was the unicorn.

Harriet therefore collected a black velvet pincushion and a

bowl of milk and honey. These she put out on the front step, politely wishing the Daughters of Night good evening, to which their only response was a baleful silence.

Next morning the milk and honey was still there. So were the Furies. Evidently they did not intend to be placated so easily. By daylight they were even less prepossessing, having black claws, bloodshot eyes, and snakes for hair. However, slipping down early to remove the saucer in case the postman tripped over it, Harriet did notice that all the pins had been removed from the pincushion. And eaten? This was encouraging. So was the fact that when the postman arrived with a card from their parents in Madeira – 'Having wonderful time hope you are behaving yourselves' – he walked clean through the Furies without noticing them at all. Evidently his conscience at least was clear.

'Perhaps they're only visible to relatives of their victims,' Harriet suggested to Mark, who was working on the unicorn horn with emery paper.

'I hope they've taken the pins to stick in Uncle Gavin,' he growled. In default of bicycle exercise Great-Uncle Gavin had made Mark do five hundred press-ups before breakfast and had personally supervised the operation. Mark felt it would be far, far better to shoot Uncle Gavin than the Furies who, after all, were only doing their duty.

The most annoying thing of all was that, after his initial interview with them, Uncle Gavin seemed not to notice the avenging spirits at all ('He only sees what he chooses to,' Harriet guessed) and walked past them quite as unconcernedly as the postman had. He packed up the golden apple in a cigar-box, rang for a taxi, and departed to London. The Furies followed him in a black, muttering group, and were seen no more for several hours; Mark and Harriet heaved sighs of relief. Prematurely, though; at tea-time the Furies reappeared, even blacker, muttering still more, and took up their post once more by the front door.

'Lost the old boy somewhere in London,' Mark diagnosed. 'Or perhaps they were chucked out of Christie's.'

The unwanted guests were certainly in a bad mood. This

time they were accompanied by a smallish thick-set winged serpent or dragon who seemed to be called Ladon. Harriet heard them saying, 'Down, Ladon! Behave yourself, and soon you shall sup on blood.' Ladon too seemed to have a snappish disposition, and nearly took off Harriet's hand when she stooped to pat him on returning home from her domestic science lesson.

'What a beautiful green his wings are. Is he yours?' she said to the Furies politely.

'He is the guardian of the apple; he but waits for his own,' Tisiphone replied dourly.

Ladon did not share the Furies' scruples about coming indoors; evidently he was used to a warmer clime and found the doorstep too draughty. He followed Harriet into the kitchen and flopped his bulky length in front of the stove, hissing cantankerously at anyone who came near, and thoroughly upsetting Walrus, the cat.

Walrus was not the only one.

'Miss Harriet! Get that nasty beast out of here at once!' exclaimed Mrs Epis, the cook, when she came back from shopping. 'And what those black ladies are doing out on the front doorstep, I'm sure *I* don't know; I've two or three times give them a hint to be off but they won't take it.'

Evidently Mrs Epis counted as one of the family or else she, too, had a guilty conscience. Mark and Harriet soon found that visitors to the house who had episodes in their past of which they had cause to be ashamed were apt to notice the Erinyes in a patchy, nervous way and hurry away with uneasy glances behind them, or else break into sudden and embarrassing confessions.

And Ladon was a thorough nuisance. So long as Harriet kept on the fan heater in her room he would lie in front of it, rolling luxuriously on his back and only snapping if anyone approached him. But at bed-time when she had turned the fan off – for she hated a warm room at night – he became fretful and roamed snarling and clanking about the house. Even Uncle Gavin tripped over him then and blamed the children furiously for leaving what he thought was a rolled-up tent lying in the passage.

41

'Things can't go on like this,' Mark said despondently.

'We've certainly got to get rid of them all somehow before Mother and Father come home next week,' Harriet agreed. 'And Uncle Gavin's plainly going to be no help at all.'

Uncle Gavin was even more tetchy than usual. Christie's had sent him a letter saying that in view of the apple's unique historical interest it was virtually impossible to put a price on it, but in their opinion it was certainly worth well over a million pounds. They would return the apple by the next registered post, pending further instructions. And the advertisement which appeared in *The Times* every day – 'Will person who persuaded young boy to exchange valuable new bicycle for metal apple on August 20 please contact Box XXX' – was producing no replies.

'Nor likely to,' Mark said. 'That chap knows when he's well out of trouble.'

During that day Mark finished his horn bow and tried shooting at the Furies with it. The operation was a total failure. The arrows, which he had after all made out of a fallow-deer's antler (brow, bay and tray), were curved and flew on a bias, like bowls, missing the visitors nine times out of ten. If they did hit they merely passed clean through and, as Mark told Harriet later, he felt a fool having to pick them up under the malign snakey-and-bonneted gaze of Alecto, Megaera and Tisiphone.

Harriet, however, came home in good spirits. She pulled out and showed Mark a paper covered with Professor Grimalkin's atrocious handwriting.

'What is it?' he asked.

'Recipe for a friendship philtre. You've heard of a love philtre? This is like that, only milder. I'm going to try it in their milk. Now don't interrupt, while I make it up.'

She put her crucible on to bubble. Mark curled up at the end of her bed and read his bird book, only coming out when Harriet tripped over Ladon and dratted him, or asked Mark's opinion about the professor's handwriting.

'Is this "verdigris" or "verjuice", do you think? And is that "Add sugar", or "Allow to simmer"?'

'It'll be a miracle if the stuff turns out all right,' Mark said pessimistically. 'Anyway, do we *want* the Furies friendly?'

'Of course we do, it'll be a tremendous help. Where was I now? Add bad egg, and brown under grill.'

Finally the potion was finished and put in a cough-mixture bottle. ('It smells awful,' Mark said, sniffing. 'Never mind, how do we know what *they* like?') A spoonful of the noxious stuff was divided between three bowls of milk, which were placed on the front step, at the feet of the unresponsive Erinyes.

However after a moment or two they began to snuff the air like bloodhounds on the track of a malefactor, and as Harriet tactfully retired she had the pleasure of seeing all three of them lapping hungrily at the mixture. So far, at least, the spell had worked. Harriet went hopefully to bed.

Next morning she was woken by a handful of earth flung at her window.

'Miss Harriet!' It was Mrs Epis on the lawn. 'Miss Harriet, you'll have to make breakfast yourself. I'm taking a week's holiday. And things had better be different when I come back or I'll give in my notice; you can tell your Ma it was me broke the Crown Derby teapot and I'm sorry about it, but there's some things a body can't bear. Now I'm off home.'

Sleepy and mystified, Harriet went to the kitchen to put on the kettle for Great-Uncle Gavin's tea. There, to her dismay, she found the Furies, who greeted her with toothy smiles. They were at ease in basket-chairs round the stove, with their long skirts turned back so as to toast their skinny legs and feet, which rested on Ladon. Roused by the indoor warmth, the snakes on their heads were in a state of disagreeable squirm and writhe, which Harriet too found hard to bear, particularly before breakfast; she quite sympathized with the cook's departure.

'Oh, good morning,' she said, however, stoutly controlling her qualms. 'Would you like some more milk?' She mixed another brew with potion (which was graciously accepted) and took up a tray of breakfast to Great-Uncle Gavin, explaining that Mrs Epis had been called away. By the time she returned,

43

Mark was in the kitchen glumly taking stock of the situation.

'Feel like a boiled egg?' Harriet said.

'I'll do it, thanks. I've had enough of your domestic science.'

They ate their boiled eggs in the garden. But they had taken only a bite or two when they were startled by hysterical screams from the window-cleaner who, having arrived early and started work on the kitchen window, had looked through the glass and was now on his knees in the flower-bed, confessing to anyone who would listen that he had pinched a diamond brooch from an upstairs bedroom in West Croydon. Before he was pacified they had also to deal with the man who came to mend the fridge, who seemed frightfully upset about something he had done to a person called Elsie, as well as a French onion-seller who dropped eight strings of onions in the back doorway and fled, crying, '*Mon Dieu, mon Dieu, mon crime est decouvert! Je suis perdu!*'

'This won't do,' said Mark, as he returned from escorting the sobbing electrician to the gate. Exhaustedly mopping his brow he didn't look where he was going, barked his shins painfully on Ladon, who was stalking the cat, and let out an oath. It went unheard; the Furies, much cheered by their breakfast and a night spent in the snug kitchen, were singing their bloodthirsty hymn fortissimo, with much clashing of tambourines. Ladon and the cat seemed all set for a duel to the death; and Great-Uncle Gavin was bawling down the stairs for less row while a man was breakfastin', dammit!

'It's all right,' Harriet soothed Mark. 'I knew the potion would work wonders. Now, your Kindlinesses,' she said to the Erinyes, 'we've got a beautiful grotto ready for you, just the sort of place you like, except I'm sorry there isn't an ilex tree, if you wouldn't mind stepping this way,' and she led them to the coal-cellar, which, being peaceful and dark, met with their entire approval.

'I daresay they'll be glad of a nap,' she remarked, shutting the door thankfully on them. 'After all, they've been unusually busy lately.'

'That's all very well,' said Mark. 'They better not stay there long. *I'm* the one that fetches the coal. And there's still beastly

Ladon to dispose of.'

Ladon, unlike his mistresses, was not tempted by milk containing a friendship potion. His nature remained as intractable as ever. He now had the cat Walrus treed on the banister post at the top of the stairs, and was coiled in a baleful bronze-and-gold heap just below, hissing like a pressure-cooker.

'Perhaps bone arrows will work on *him*,' said Mark, and dashed to his bedroom.

As he reappeared a lot of things happened at once.

The postman rang the front-door bell and handed Harriet a letter for Uncle Gavin and a registered parcel labelled GOLD WITH CARE. Ladon made a dart at the cat, who countered with a faster-than-light left hook, all claws extended. It caught the dragon in his gills and he let out a screech like the whistle of a steam locomotive, which fetched the Furies from their grotto at the double, brass-studded batons out and snakes ready to strike.

At the same moment Mark let fly with his bow and arrow and Uncle Gavin burst from his bedroom exclaiming, 'I *will* not have this bedlam while I'm digestin' my breakfast!' He received the arrow intended for Ladon full in his slippered heel and gave a yell which quite drowned the noise made by the cat and dragon.

'Who did that? Who fired that damned thing?' Enraged, hopping, Uncle Gavin pulled out the bone dart. 'What's that cat doin' up there? Why's this confounded reptile in the house? Who are those people down there? *What the devil's going on around here?*'

Harriet gave a shout of joy.

'Look, quick!' she called to the Furies. 'Look at his heel! It's bleeding!' (It was indeed.) 'You said blood had to flow and now it has, so you've done your job and can leave with clear consciences! Quick, Mark, open the parcel and give that wretched dragon his apple and they can *all* leave. Poor Uncle Gavin, is your foot very painful? Mark didn't mean to hit you. I'll bandage it up in two shakes.'

Mark tore the parcel undone and tossed the golden apple to Ladon, who caught it with a snap of his jaws and was gone in a

45

flash through the landing window. (It was shut, but no matter.) At the same moment the Furies, their lust for vengeance appeased by the sight of Uncle Gavin's gore, departed with more dignity by the front door.

Alecto even turned and gave Harriet a ghastly smile.

'Thank you for having us, child,' she said. 'We enjoyed our visit.'

'Don't mention it,' Harriet mechanically replied, and only just stopped herself from adding, 'Come again.'

Then she sat her great-uncle in the kitchen armchair and bathed his heel. The wound, luckily, proved to be no more than a scratch. While she bandaged it he read his letter, and suddenly gave a curious grunt, of pleasure and astonishment.

'God bless my soul! They want me back! Would you believe it!'

'Who wants you back, Great-Uncle?' Harriet asked, tying the ends of the bandage in a knot.

'The Mbutam-Mbutas, bless 'em! They want me to go and help 'em as Military and Economic Adviser. I've always said there's good in the black feller and I say so yet! Well, well, well! Don't know when I've been so pleased.' He gave his nose a tremendous blow and wiped his eyes.

'Oh, Uncle Gavin, how perfectly splendid!' Harriet gave him a hug. 'When do they want you to go?'

'Three weeks' time. Bless my soul, I'll have a bustle getting me kit ready.'

'Oh, we'll all help like mad. I'll run down the road now and fetch Mrs Epis; I'm sure she'll be glad to come back for such an emergency.'

Mrs Epis had no objection at all, once she was assured the intruders were gone from the house.

Harriet had one startled moment when they got back to the house.

'Uncle Gavin!' she called, and ran upstairs. The old gentleman had out his tin tropical trunk and was inspecting a pith helmet. 'Yes, m'dear, what is it?' he said absently.

'The little brown bottle on the kitchen table. Was it – did you – you –?'

'Oh, that? My cough mixture? Yes, I finished it and threw the bottle away. Why, though, bless my soul – *there's* my cough mixture! What the deuce have I been an' taken, then, gel? Anything harmful?'

'Oh no, perfectly harmless,' Harriet hastily reassured him. 'Now, you give me anything you want mended and I'll be getting on with it.'

''Pon my soul,' Uncle Gavin said, pulling out a bundle of spotless white ducks and a dress-jacket with tremendous epaulettes and fringes, ''pon my soul, I believe I'll miss you young ones when I'm back in the tropics. Come and visit me sometimes, m'dear? Young Mark too. Where is the young rogue? Ho, ho, can't help laughing when I think how he hit me in the heel. Who'd have thought he had it in him?'

'He's gone apple-picking at the farm down the road,' Harriet explained. 'He wants to earn enough to pay back that thirty-five pounds.'

'Good lad, good lad!' Uncle Gavin exclaimed approvingly. 'Not that he need have bothered, mark you.'

And in fact, when Mark tried to press the money on Uncle Gavin at his departure, he would have none of it.

'No, no, bless your little hearts, split it between you.' He chucked Harriet under the chin and earnestly shook Mark's hand. 'I'd never have thought I'd cotton to young 'uns as I have to you two – 'mazing thing. So you keep the money and buy something pretty to remind you of my visit.'

But Mark and Harriet thought they would remember his visit quite easily without that – especially as the Furies had taken quite a fancy to the coal-cellar and frequently came back to occupy it on chilly winter nights.

Memories of Christmas

DYLAN THOMAS

One Christmas was so much like another, in those years, around the sea-town corner now, and out of all sound except the distant speaking of the voices I sometimes hear a moment before sleep, that I can never remember whether it snowed for six days and six nights when I was twelve or whether it snowed for twelve days and twelve nights when I was six; or whether the ice broke and the skating grocer vanished like a snowman through a white trap-door on that same Christmas Day that the mince-pies finished Uncle Arnold and we tobogganed down the seaward hill, all the afternoon, on the best tea-tray, and Mrs Griffiths complained, and we threw a snowball at her niece, and my hands burned so, with the heat and the cold, when I held them in front of the fire, that I cried for twenty minutes and then had some jelly.

All the Christmases roll down the hill towards the Welsh-speaking sea, like a snowball growing whiter and bigger and rounder, like a cold and headlong moon bundling down the sky that was our street; and they stop at the rim of the ice-edged, fish-freezing waves, and I plunge my hands in the snow and bring out whatever I can find; holly or robins or pudding, squabbles and carols and oranges and tin whistles, and the fire in the front room, and bang go the crackers, and holy, holy, holy, ring the bells, and the glass bells shaking on the tree, and Mother Goose, and Struwelpeter – oh! the baby-burning flames and the clacking scissorman! – Billy Bunter and Black Beauty, Little Women and boys who have three helpings, Alice and Mrs Potter's badgers, penknives, teddy-bears – named after a Mr Theodore Bear, their inventor, or father, who died recently in the United States – mouth-organs, tin-soldiers, and blancmange, and Auntie Bessie playing 'Pop Goes the Weasel' and 'Nuts in May' and 'Oranges and Lemons' on

the untuned piano in the parlour all through the thimble-hiding musical-chairing blind-man's-buffing party at the end of the never-to-be-forgotten day at the end of the unremembered year.

In goes my hand into that wool-white bell-tongued ball of holidays resting at the margin of the carol-singing sea, and out come Mrs Prothero and the firemen.

It was on the afternoon of the day of Christmas Eve, and I was in Mrs Prothero's garden, waiting for cats, with her son Jim. It was snowing. It was always snowing at Christmas; December, in my memory, is white as Lapland, though there were no reindeers. But there were cats. Patient, cold, and callous, our hands wrapped in socks, we waited to snowball the cats. Sleek and long as jaguars and terrible-whiskered, spitting and snarling they would slink and sidle over the white back-garden walls, and the lynx-eyed hunters, Jim and I, fur-capped and moccasined trappers from Hudson's Bay off Eversley Road, would hurl our deadly snowballs at the green of their eyes. The wise cats never appeared. We were so still, Eskimo-footed arctic marksmen in the muffling silence of the eternal snows – eternal, ever since Wednesday – that we never heard Mrs Prothero's first cry from her igloo at the bottom of the garden. Or, if we heard it at all, it was, to us, like the far-off challenge of our enemy and prey, the neighbour's Polar Cat. But soon the voice grew louder. 'Fire!' cried Mrs Prothero, and she beat the dinner-gong. And we ran down the garden, with the snowballs in our arms, towards the house, and smoke, indeed, was pouring out of the dining-room, and the gong was bombilating, and Mrs Prothero was announcing ruin like a town-crier in Pompeii. This was better than all the cats in Wales standing on the wall in a row. We bounded into the house, laden with snowballs, and stopped at the open door of the smoke-filled room. Something was burning all right; perhaps it was Mr Prothero, who always slept there after midday dinner with a newspaper over his face; but he was standing in the middle of the room, saying 'A fine Christmas!' and smacking at the smoke with a slipper.

'Call the fire-brigade,' cried Mrs Prothero as she beat the gong.

'They won't be there,' said Mr Prothero, 'it's Christmas.'

There was no fire to be seen, only clouds of smoke and Mr Prothero standing in the middle of them, waving his slipper as though he were conducting.

'Do something,' he said.

And we threw all our snowballs into the smoke – I think we missed Mr Prothero – and ran out of the house to the telephone-box.

'Let's call the police as well,' Jim said.

'And the ambulance.'

'And Ernie Jenkins, he likes fires.'

But we only called the fire-brigade, and soon the fire-engine came and three tall men in helmets brought a hose into the house and Mr Prothero got out just in time before they turned it on. Nobody could have had a noisier Christmas Eve. And when the firemen turned off the hose and were standing in the wet and smoky room, Jim's aunt, Miss Prothero, came downstairs and peered in at them. Jim and I waited, very quietly, to hear what she would say to them. She said the right thing, always. She looked at the three tall firemen in their shining helmets, standing among the smoke and cinders and dissolving snowballs, and she said: 'Would you like something to read?'

Now out of that bright white snowball of Christmas gone comes the stocking, the stocking of stockings, that hung at the foot of the bed with the arm of a golliwog dangling over the top and small bells ringing in the toes. There was a company, gallant and scarlet but never nice to taste though I always tried when very young, of belted and busbied and musketed lead soldiers so soon to lose their heads and legs in the wars on the kitchen table after the tea-things, the mince-pies, and the cakes that I helped to make by stoning the raisins and eating them, had been cleared away; and a bag of moist and many-coloured jelly-babies and a folded flag and a false nose and a tram-conductor's cap and a machine that punched tickets and rang a bell; never a catapult; once, by a mistake that no one could explain, a little hatchet; and a rubber buffalo, or it may have been a horse, with a yellow head and haphazard legs; and a celluloid duck that made, when you pressed it, a most unducklike noise, a mewing moo that an ambitious cat might make who wishes to be a cow; and a painting-book in which I could make the grass, the trees, the sea, and the animals any colour I pleased: and still the dazzling sky-blue sheep are grazing in the red field under a flight of rainbow-beaked and pea-green birds.

Christmas morning was always over before you could say Jack Frost. And look! suddenly the pudding was burning! Bang the gong and call the fire-brigade and the book-loving firemen! Someone found the silver threepenny-bit with a currant on it; and the someone was always Uncle Arnold. The motto in my cracker read:

Let's all have fun this Christmas Day,
Let's play and sing and shout hooray!

and the grown-ups turned their eyes towards the ceiling, and Auntie Bessie, who had already been frightened, twice, by a clockwork mouse, whimpered at the sideboard and had some elderberry wine. And someone put a glass bowl full of nuts on the littered table, and my uncle said, as he said once every year: 'I've got a shoe-nut here. Fetch me a shoe-horn to open it, boy.'

And dinner was ended.

And I remember that on the afternoon of Christmas Day, when the others sat around the fire and told each other that this was nothing, no, nothing, to the great snowbound and turkey-proud yule-log-crackling holly-berry-bedizined and kissing-under-the-mistletoe Christmas when *they* were children, I would go out, school-capped and gloved and mufflered, with my bright new boots squeaking, into the white world on to the seaward hill, to call on Jim and Dan and Jack and to walk with them through the silent snowscape of our town.

We went padding through the streets, leaving huge deep footprints in the snow, on the hidden pavements.

'I bet people'll think there's been hippoes.'

'What would you do if you saw a hippo coming down Terrace Road?'

'I'd go like this, bang! I'd throw him over the railings and

52

roll him down the hill and then I'd tickle him under the ear and he'd wag his tail . . .'

'What would you do if you saw *two* hippoes . . .?'

Iron-flanked and bellowing he-hippoes clanked and blundered and battered through the scudding snow towards us as we passed by Mr Daniel's house.

'Let's post Mr Daniel a snowball through his letterbox.'

'Let's write things in the snow.'

'Let's write "Mr Daniel looks like a spaniel" all over his lawn.'

'Look,' Jack said, 'I'm eating snow-pie.'

'What's it taste like?'

'Like snow-pie,' Jack said.

Or we walked on the white shore.

'Can the fishes see it's snowing?'

'They think it's the sky falling down.'

The silent one-clouded heavens drifted on to the sea.

'All the old dogs have gone.'

Dogs of a hundred mingled makes yapped in the summer at the sea-rim and yelped at the trespassing mountains of the waves.

'I bet St Bernards would like it now.'

And we were snowblind travellers lost on the north hills, and the great dewlapped dogs, with brandy-flasks round their necks, ambled and shambled up to us, baying 'Excelsior'.

We returned home through the desolate poor sea-facing streets where only a few children fumbled with bare red fingers in the thick wheel-rutted snow and catcalled after us, their voices fading away, as we trudged uphill, into the cries of the dock-birds and the hooters of ships out in the white and whirling bay.

Bring out the tall tales now that we told by the fire as we roasted chestnuts and the gaslight bubbled low. Ghosts with their heads under their arms trailed their chains and said 'whooo' like owls in the long nights when I dared not look over my shoulder; wild beasts lurked in the cubby-hole under the stairs where the gas-meter ticked. 'Once upon a time,' Jim said, 'there were three boys, just like us, who got lost in the dark in the snow, near Bethesda Chapel, and this is what happened to them. . . .' It was the most dreadful happening I had ever heard.

And I remember that we went singing carols once, a night or two before Christmas Eve, when there wasn't the shaving of a moon to light the secret, white-flying streets. At the end of a long road was a drive that led to a large house, and we stumbled up the darkness of the drive that night, each one of us afraid, each one holding a stone in his hand in case, and all of us too brave to say a word. The wind made through the drive-trees noises as of old and unpleasant and maybe web-footed men wheezing in caves. We reached the black bulk of the house.

'What shall we give them?' Dan whispered.

'"Hark the Herald"? "Christmas comes but Once a Year"?'

'No,' Jack said: 'We'll sing "Good King Wenceslas." I'll count three.'

One, two, three, and we began to sing, our voices high and seemingly distant in the snow-felted darkness round the house that was occupied by nobody we knew. We stood close together, near the dark door.

Good King Wenceslas looked out
On the Feast of Stephen.

And then a small, dry voice, like the voice of someone who has not spoken for a long time, suddenly joined our singing: a small, dry voice from the other side of the door: a small, dry voice through the keyhole. And when we stopped running we were outside *our* house; the front room was lovely and bright; the gramophone was playing; we saw the red and white balloons hanging from the gas-bracket; uncles and aunts sat by the fire; I thought I smelt our supper being fried in the kitchen. Everything was good again, and Christmas shone through all the familiar town.

'Perhaps it was a ghost,' Jim said.

'Perhaps it was trolls,' Dan said, who was always reading.

'Let's go in and see if there's any jelly left,' Jack said. And we did that.

54

The Lumber-Room

SAKI

The children were to be driven, as a special treat, to the sands at Jagborough. Nicholas was not to be of the party; he was in disgrace. Only that morning he had refused to eat his wholesome bread-and-milk on the seemingly frivolous ground that there was a frog in it. Older and wiser and better people had told him that there could not possibly be a frog in his bread-and-milk and that he was not to talk nonsense; he continued, nevertheless, to talk what seemed the veriest nonsense, and described with much detail the coloration and markings of the alleged frog. The dramatic part of the incident was that there really was a frog in Nicholas' basin of bread-and-milk; he had put it there himself, so he felt entitled to know something about it. The sin of taking a frog from the garden and putting it into a bowl of wholesome bread-and-milk was enlarged on at great length, but the fact that stood out clearest in the whole affair, as it presented itself to the mind of Nicholas, was that the older, wiser, and better people had been proved to be profoundly in error in matters about which they had expressed the utmost assurance.

'You said there couldn't possibly be a frog in my bread-and-milk; there *was* a frog in my bread-and-milk,' he repeated, with the insistence of a skilled tactician who does not intend to shift from favourable ground.

So his boy-cousin and girl-cousin and his quite uninteresting younger brother were to be taken to Jagborough sands that afternoon and he was to stay at home. His cousins' aunt, who insisted, by an unwarranted stretch of imagination, in styling herself his aunt also, had hastily invented the Jagborough expedition in order to impress on Nicholas the delights that he had justly forfeited by his disgraceful conduct at the breakfast-table. It was her habit, whenever one of the children fell from

55

grace, to improvise something of a festival nature from which the offender would be rigorously debarred; if all the children sinned collectively they were suddenly informed of a circus in a neighbouring town, a circus of unrivalled merit and uncounted elephants, to which, but for their depravity, they would have been taken that very day.

A few decent tears were looked for on the part of Nicholas when the moment for the departure of the expedition arrived. As a matter of fact, however, all the crying was done by his girl-cousin, who scraped her knee rather painfully against the step of the carriage as she was scrambling in.

'How she did howl,' said Nicholas cheerfully, as the party drove off without any of the elation of high spirits that should have characterized it.

'She'll soon get over that,' said the *soi-disant* aunt; 'it will be a glorious afternoon for racing about over those beautiful sands. How they will enjoy themselves!'

'Bobby won't enjoy himself much, and he won't race much either,' said Nicholas with a grim chuckle; 'his boots are hurting him. They're too tight.'

'Why didn't he tell me they were hurting?' asked the aunt with some asperity.

'He told you twice, but you weren't listening. You often don't listen when we tell you important things.'

'You are not to go into the gooseberry garden,' said the aunt, changing the subject.

'Why not?' demanded Nicholas.

'Because you are in disgrace,' said the aunt loftily.

Nicholas did not admit the flawlessness of the reasoning; he felt perfectly capable of being in disgrace and in a gooseberry garden at the same moment. His face took on an expression of considerable obstinacy. It was clear to his aunt that he was determined to get into the gooseberry garden, 'only,' as she remarked to herself, 'because I have told him he is not to.'

Now the gooseberry garden had two doors by which it might be entered, and once a small person like Nicholas could slip in there he could effectually disappear from view amid the masking growth of artichokes, raspberry canes, and fruit bushes. The aunt had many other things to do that afternoon, but she spent an hour or two in trivial gardening operations among flower beds and shrubberies, whence she could keep a watchful eye on the two doors that led to the forbidden paradise. She was a woman of few ideas, with immense powers of concentration.

Nicholas made one or two sorties into the front garden, wriggling his way with obvious stealth of purpose towards one or other of the doors, but never able for a moment to evade the aunt's watchful eye. As a matter of fact, he had no intention of trying to get into the gooseberry garden, but it was extremely convenient for him that his aunt should believe that he had; it was a belief that would keep her on self-imposed sentry-duty for the greater part of the afternoon. Having thoroughly confirmed and fortified her suspicions, Nicholas slipped back into the house and rapidly put into execution a plan of action that had long germinated in his brain. By standing on a chair in the library one could reach a shelf on which reposed a fat, important-looking key. The key was as important as it looked; it was the instrument which kept the mysteries of the lumber-room secure from unauthorized intrusion, which opened a way only for aunts and such-like privileged persons. Nicholas had not had much experience of the art of fitting keys into keyholes and turning locks, but for some days past he had practised with the key of the school-room door; he did not believe in trusting too much to luck and accident. The key turned stiffly in the lock, but it turned. The door opened, and Nicholas was in an unknown land, compared with which the gooseberry garden was a stale delight, a mere material pleasure.

Often and often Nicholas had pictured to himself what the lumber-room might be like, that region that was so carefully sealed from youthful eyes and concerning which no questions were ever answered. It came up to his expectations. In the first place it was large and dimly lit, one high window opening on to the forbidden garden being its only source of illumination. In the second place it was a storehouse of unimagined treasures. The aunt-by-assertion was one of those people who think that things spoil by use and consign them to dust and damp by way

of preserving them. Such parts of the house as Nicholas knew best were rather bare and cheerless, but here there were wonderful things for the eye to feast on. First and foremost there was a piece of framed tapestry that was evidently meant to be a fire-screen. To Nicholas it was a living, breathing story; he sat down on a roll of Indian hangings, glowing in wonderful colours beneath a layer of dust, and took in all the details of the tapestry picture. A man, dressed in the hunting costume of some remote period, had just transfixed a stag with an arrow; it could not have been a difficult shot because the stag was only one or two paces away from him; in the thickly growing vegetation that the picture suggested it would not have been difficult to creep up to a feeding stag, and the two spotted dogs that were springing forward to join in the chase had evidently been trained to keep to heel till the arrow was discharged. That part of the picture was simple, if interesting, but did the huntsman see, what Nicholas saw, that four galloping wolves were coming in his direction through the wood? There might be more than four of them hidden behind the trees, and in any case would the man and his dogs be able to cope with the four wolves if they made an attack? The man had only two arrows left in his quiver, and he might miss with one or both of them; all one knew about his skill in shooting was that he could hit a large stag at a ridiculously short range. Nicholas sat for many golden minutes revolving the possibilities of the scene; he was inclined to think that there were more than four wolves and that the man and his dogs were in a tight corner.

But there were other objects of delight and interest claiming his instant attention; there were quaint twisted candlesticks in the shape of snakes, and a teapot fashioned like a china duck, out of whose open beak the tea was supposed to come. How dull and shapeless the nursery teapot seemed in comparison! And there was a carved sandal-wood box packed tight with aromatic cotton-wool, and between the layers of cotton-wool were little brass figures, hump-necked bulls, and peacocks and goblins, delightful to see and to handle. Less promising in appearance was a large square book with plain black covers; Nicholas peeped into it, and, behold, it was full of coloured pictures of birds. And such birds! In the garden, and in the lanes when he went for a walk, Nicholas came across a few birds, of which the largest were an occasional magpie or wood-pigeon; here were herons and bustards, kites, toucans, tiger-bitterns, brush turkeys, ibises, golden pheasants, a whole portrait gallery of undreamed-of creatures. And as he was admiring the colouring of the mandarin duck and assigning a life-history to it, the voice of his aunt in shrill vociferation of his name came from the gooseberry garden without. She had grown suspicious at his long disappearance, and had leapt to the conclusion that he had climbed over the wall behind the sheltering screen of the lilac bushes; she was now engaged in energetic and rather hopeless search for him among the artichokes and raspberry canes.

'Nicholas, Nicholas!' she screamed, 'you are to come out of this at once. It's no use trying to hide there; I can see you all the time.'

It was probably the first time for twenty years that any one had smiled in that lumber-room.

Presently the angry repetitions of Nicholas' name gave way to a shriek, and a cry for somebody to come quickly. Nicholas shut the book, restored it carefully to its place in a corner, and shook some dust from a neighbouring pile of newspapers over it. Then he crept from the room, locked the door, and replaced the key exactly where he had found it. His aunt was still calling his name when he sauntered into the front garden.

'Who's calling?' he asked.

'Me,' came the answer from the other side of the wall, 'didn't you hear me? I've been looking for you in the goose-berry garden, and I've slipped into the rain-water tank. Luckily there's no water in it, but the sides are slippery and I can't get out. Fetch the little ladder from under the cherry tree –'

'I was told I wasn't to go into the gooseberry garden,' said Nicholas promptly.

'I told you not to, and now I tell you that you may,' came the voice from the rain-water tank, rather impatiently.

'Your voice doesn't sound like aunt's,' objected Nicholas,

'you may be the Evil One tempting me to be disobedient. Aunt often tells me that the Evil One tempts me and that I always yield. This time I'm not going to yield.'

'Don't talk nonsense,' said the prisoner in the tank; 'go and fetch the ladder.'

'Will there be strawberry jam for tea?' asked Nicholas innocently.

'Certainly there will be,' said the aunt, privately resolving that Nicholas should have none of it.

'Now I know that you are the Evil One and not aunt,' shouted Nicholas gleefully; 'when we asked aunt for strawberry jam yesterday she said there wasn't any. I know there are four jars of it in the store cupboard, because I looked, and of course you know it's there, but *she* doesn't, because she said there wasn't any. Oh, Devil, you *have* sold yourself!'

There was an unusual sense of luxury in being able to talk to an aunt as though one was talking to the Evil One, but Nicholas knew, with childish discernment, that such luxuries were not to be over-indulged in. He walked noisily away, and it was a kitchenmaid, in search of parsley, who eventually rescued the aunt from the rain-water tank.

Tea that evening was partaken of in a fearsome silence. The tide had been at its highest when the children had arrived at Jagborough Cove, so there had been no sands to play on – a circumstance that the aunt had overlooked in the haste of organizing her punitive expedition. The tightness of Bobby's boots had had disastrous effect on his temper the whole of the afternoon, and altogether the children could not have been said to have enjoyed themselves. The aunt maintained the frozen muteness of one who has suffered undignified and unmerited detention in a rain-water tank for thirty-five minutes. As for Nicholas, he, too, was silent, in the absorption of one who has much to think about; it was just possible, he considered, that the huntsman would escape with his hounds while the wolves feasted on the stricken stag.

61

The Doll's House

KATHERINE MANSFIELD

When dear old Mrs Hay went back to town after staying with
the Burnells she sent the children a doll's house. It was so big
that the carter and Pat carried it into the courtyard, and there
it stayed, propped up on two wooden boxes beside the feed-
room door. No harm could come to it; it was summer. And
perhaps the smell of paint would have gone off by the time it
had to be taken in. For, really, the smell of paint coming from
that doll's house ('Sweet of old Mrs Hay, of course; most sweet
and generous!') – but the smell of paint was quite enough to
make anyone seriously ill, in Aunt Beryl's opinion. Even
before the sacking was taken off. And when it was . . .

There stood the doll's house, a dark, oily, spinach green,
picked out with bright yellow. Its two solid little chimneys,
glued on to the roof, were painted red and white, and the door,
gleaming with yellow varnish, was like a little slab of toffee.
Four windows, real windows, were divided into panes by a
broad streak of green. There was actually a tiny porch, too,
painted yellow, with big lumps of congealed paint hanging
along the edge.

But perfect, perfect little house! Who could possibly mind
the smell. It was part of the joy, part of the newness.

'Open it quickly, someone!'

The hook at the side was stuck fast. Pat prised it open with
his penknife, and the whole house front swung back, and –
there you were, gazing at one and the same moment into the
drawing-room and dining-room, the kitchen and two bed-
rooms. That is the way for a house to open! Why don't all
houses open like that? How much more exciting than peering
through the slit of a door into a mean little hall with a hat-stand
and two umbrellas! That is – isn't it? – what you long to know
about a house when you put your hand on the knocker.

Perhaps it is the way God opens houses at the dead of night when He is taking a quiet turn with an angel. . . .

'Oh-oh!' the Burnell children sounded as though they were in despair. It was too marvellous; it was too much for them. They had never seen anything like it in their lives. All the rooms were papered. There were pictures on the walls, painted on the paper, with gold frames complete. Red carpet covered all the floors except the kitchen; red plush chairs in the drawing-room, green in the dining-room; tables, beds with real bedclothes, a cradle, a stove, a dresser with tiny plates and one big jug. But what Kezia liked more than anything, what she liked frightfully, was the lamp. It stood in the middle of the dining-room table, an exquisite little amber lamp with a white globe. It was even filled all ready for lighting, though, of course, you couldn't light it. But there was something inside that looked like oil and moved when you shook it.

The father and mother dolls, who sprawled very stiff as though they had fainted in the drawing-room, and their two little children asleep upstairs, were really too big for the doll's house. They didn't look as though they belonged. But the lamp was perfect. It seemed to smile at Kezia, to say, 'I live here.' The lamp was real.

The Brunell children could hardly walk to school fast enough the next morning. They burned to tell everybody, to describe, to – well – to boast about their doll's house before the school-bell rang.

'I'm to tell,' said Isabel, 'because I'm the eldest. And you two can join in after. But I'm to tell first.'

There was nothing to answer. Isabel was bossy, but she was always right, and Lottie and Kezia knew too well the powers that went with being eldest. They brushed through the thick buttercups at the road edge and said nothing.

'And I'm to choose who's to come and see it first. Mother said I might.'

For it had been arranged that while the doll's house stood in the courtyard they might ask the girls at school, two at a time, to come and look. Not to stay to tea, of course, or to come traipsing through the house. But just to stand quietly in the courtyard while Isabel pointed out the beauties, and Lottie and Kezia looked pleased. . . .

But hurry as they might, by the time they had reached the tarred palings of the boys' playground the bell had begun to jangle. They only just had time to whip off their hats and fall into line before the roll was called. Never mind. Isabel tried to make up for it by looking very important and mysterious and by whispering behind her hand to the girls near her, 'Got something to tell you at playtime.'

Playtime came and Isabel was surrounded. The girls of her class nearly fought to put their arms round her, to walk away with her, to beam flatteringly, to be her special friend. She held quite a court under the huge pine trees at the side of the playground. Nudging, giggling together, the little girls pressed up close. And the only two who stayed outside the ring were the two who were always outside, the little Kelveys. They knew better than to come anywhere near the Burnells.

For the fact was, the school the Burnell children went to was not at all the kind of place their parents would have chosen if there had been any choice. But there was none. It was the only school for miles. And the consequence was all the children of the neighbourhood, the Judge's little girls, the doctor's daughters, the store-keeper's children, the milkman's, were forced to mix together. Not to speak of there being an equal number of rude, rough little boys as well. But the line had to be drawn somewhere. It was drawn at the Kelveys. Many of the children, including the Burnells, were not allowed even to speak to them. They walked past the Kelveys with their heads in the air, and as they set the fashion in all matters of behaviour, the Kelveys were shunned by everybody. Even the teacher had a special voice for them, and a special smile for the other children when Lil Kelvey came up to her desk with a bunch of dreadfully common-looking flowers.

They were the daughters of a spry, hard-working little washerwoman, who went about from house to house by the day. This was awful enough. But where was Mr Kelvey? Nobody knew for certain. But everybody said he was in prison.

So they were the daughters of a washerwoman and a gaolbird. Very nice company for other people's children! And they looked it. Why Mrs Kelvey made them so conspicuous was hard to understand. The truth was they were dressed in 'bits' given to her by the people for whom she worked. Lil, for instance, who was a stout, plain child, with big freckles, came to school in a dress made from a green art-serge tablecloth of the Burnells', with red plush sleeves from the Logans' curtains. Her hat, perched on top of her high forehead, was a grown-up woman's hat, once the property of Miss Lecky, the postmistress. It was turned up at the back and trimmed with a large scarlet quill. What a little guy she looked! It was impossible not to laugh. And her little sister, our Else, wore a long white dress, rather like a nightgown, and a pair of little boy's boots. But whatever our Else wore she would have looked strange. She was a tiny wishbone of a child, with cropped hair and enormous solemn eyes – a little white owl. Nobody had ever seen her smile; she scarcely ever spoke. She went through life holding on to Lil, with a piece of Lil's skirt screwed up in her hand. Where Lil went, our Else followed. In the playground, on the road going to and from school, there was Lil marching in front and our Else holding on behind. Only when she wanted anything, or when she was out of breath, our Else gave Lil a tug, a twitch, and Lil stopped and turned round. The Kelveys never failed to understand each other.

Now they hovered at the edge; you couldn't stop them listening. When the little girls turned round and sneered, Lil, as usual, gave her silly, shamefaced smile, but our Else only looked.

And Isabel's voice, so very proud, went on telling. The carpet made a great sensation, but so did the beds with real bedclothes, and the stove with an oven door.

When she finished Kezia broke in. 'You've forgotten the lamp, Isabel.'

'Oh yes,' said Isabel, 'and there's a teeny little lamp, all made of yellow glass, with a white globe that stands on the dining-room table. You couldn't tell it from a real one.'

'The lamp's best of all,' cried Kezia. She thought Isabel

wasn't making half enough of the little lamp. But nobody paid any attention. Isabel was choosing the two who were to come back with them that afternoon and see it. She chose Emmie Cole and Lena Logan. But when the others knew they were all to have a chance, they couldn't be nice enough to Isabel. One by one they put their arms round Isabel's waist and walked her off. They had something to whisper to her, a secret. 'Isabel's *my* friend.'

Only the little Kelveys moved away forgotten; there was nothing more for them to hear.

Days passed, and as more children saw the doll's house, the fame of it spread. It became the one subject, the rage. The one question was, 'Have you seen Burnells' doll's house? Oh, ain't it lovely!' 'Haven't you seen it? Oh, I say!'

Even the dinner hour was given up to talking about it. The litle girls sat under the pines eating their thick mutton sandwiches and big slabs of johnny cake spread with butter. While always, as near as they could get, sat the Kelveys, our Else holding on to Lil, listening too, while they chewed their jam sandwiches out of a newspaper soaked with large red blobs.

'Mother,' said Kezia, 'can't I ask the Kelveys just once?'

'Certainly not, Kezia.'

'But why not?'

'Run away, Kezia; you know quite well why not.'

At last everybody had seen it except them. On that day the subject rather flagged. It was the dinner hour. The children stood together under the pine trees, and suddenly, as they looked at the Kelveys eating out of their paper, always by themselves, always listening, they wanted to be horrid to them. Emmie Cole started the whisper.

'Lil Kelvey's going to be a servant when she grows up.'

'O-oh, how awful!' said Isabel Burnell, and she made eyes at Emmie.

Emmie swallowed in a very meaning way and nodded to Isabel as she'd seen her mother do on those occasions.

'It's true – it's true – it's true,' she said.

Then Lena Logan's little eyes snapped. 'Shall I ask her?' she whispered.

'Bet you don't,' said Jessie May.

'Pooh, I'm not frightened,' said Lena. Suddenly she gave a little squeal and danced in front of the other girls. 'Watch! Watch me! Watch me now!' said Lena. And sliding, gliding, dragging one foot, giggling behind her hand, Lena went over to the Kelveys.

Lil looked up from her dinner. She wrapped the rest quickly away. Our Else stopped chewing. What was coming now?

'Is it true you're going to be a servant when you grow up, Lil Kelvey?' shrilled Lena.

Dead silence. But instead of answering, Lil only gave her silly, shamefaced smile. She didn't seem to mind the question at all. What a sell for Lena! The girls began to titter.

Lena couldn't stand that. She put her hands on her hips; she shot forward. 'Yah, yer father's in prison!' she hissed spitefully.

This was such a marvellous thing to have said that the little girls rushed away in a body, deeply, deeply excited, wild with joy. Someone found a long rope, and they began skipping. And never did they skip so high, run in and out so fast, or do such daring things as on that morning.

In the afternoon Pat called for the Burnell children with the buggy and they drove home. There were visitors. Isabel and Lottie, who liked visitors, went upstairs to change their pinafores. But Kezia thieved out at the back. Nobody was about; she began to swing on the big white gates of the courtyard. Presently, looking along the road, she saw two little dots. They grew bigger, they were coming towards her. Now she could see that one was in front and one close behind. Now she could see that they were the Kelveys. Kezia stopped swinging. She slipped off the gate as if she was going to run away. Then she hesitated. The Kelveys came nearer, and beside them walked their shadows, very long, stretching right across the road with their heads in the buttercups. Kezia clambered back on the gate; she had made up her mind; she swung out.

'Hullo,' she said to the passing Kelveys.

They were so astounded that they stopped. Lil gave her silly smile. Our Else stared.

'You can come and see our doll's house if you want to,' said Kezia, and she dragged one toe on the ground. But at that Lil turned red and shook her head quickly.

'Why not?' asked Kezia.

Lil gasped, then she said, 'Your ma told our ma you wasn't to speak to us.'

'Oh, well,' said Kezia. She didn't know what to reply. 'It doesn't matter. You can come and see our doll's house all the same. Come on. Nobody's looking.'

But Lil shook her head still harder.

'Don't you want to?' asked Kezia.

Suddenly there was a twitch, a tug at Lil's skirt. She turned round. Our Else was looking at her with big, imploring eyes; she was frowning; she wanted to go. For a moment Lil looked at our Else very doubtfully. But then our Else twitched her skirt again. She started forward. Kezia led the way. Like two little stray cats they followed across the courtyard to where the doll's house stood.

'There it is,' said Kezia.

There was a pause. Lil breathed loudly, almost snorted; our Else was still as stone.

'I'll open it for you,' said Kezia kindly. She undid the hook and they looked inside.

'There's the drawing-room and the dining-room, and that's the –'

'Kezia!'

Oh, what a start they gave!

'Kezia!'

It was Aunt Beryl's voice. They turned round. At the back door stood Aunt Beryl, staring as if she couldn't believe what she saw.

'How dare you ask the little Kelveys into the courtyard!' said her cold, furious voice. 'You know as well as I do, you're not allowed to talk to them. Run away, children, run away at once. And don't come back again,' said Aunt Beryl. And she stepped into the yard and shooed them out as if they were chickens.

'Off you go immediately!' she called, cold and proud.

They did not need telling twice. Burning with shame, shrinking together, Lil huddling along like her mother, our Else dazed, somehow they crossed the big courtyard and squeezed through the white gate.

'Wicked, disobedient little girl!' said Aunt Beryl bitterly to Kezia, and she slammed the doll's house to.

The afternoon had been awful. A letter had come from Willie Brent, a terrifying, threatening letter, saying if she did not meet him that evening in Pulman's Bush, he'd come to the front door and ask the reason why! But now that she had frightened those little rats of Kelveys and given Kezia a good scolding, her heart felt lighter. That ghastly pressure was gone. She went back to the house humming.

When the Kelveys were well out of sight of Burnells', they sat down to rest on a big red drainpipe by the side of the road. Lil's cheeks were still burning; she took off the hat with the quill and held it on her knee. Dreamily they looked over the hay paddocks, past the creek, to the group of wattles where Logan's cows stood waiting to be milked. What were their thoughts?

Presently our Else nudged up close to her sister. But now she had forgotten the cross lady. She put out a finger and stroked her sister's quill; she smiled her rare smile.

'I seen the little lamp,' she said softly.

Then both were silent once more.

Enchanted Alley

MICHAEL ANTHONY

Leaving for school early on mornings, I walked slowly through the busy parts of the town. The business places would all be opening then and smells of strange fragrance would fill the High Street. Inside the opening doors I would see clerks dusting, arranging, hanging things up, getting ready for the day's business. They looked cheerful and eager and they opened the doors very wide. Sometimes I stood up to watch them.

In places between the stores several little alleys ran off the High Street. Some were busy and some were not and there was one that was long and narrow and dark and very strange. Here, too, the shops would be opening as I passed and there would be bearded Indians in loin-cloths spreading rugs on the pavement. There would be Indian women also, with veils thrown over their shoulders, setting up their stalls and chatting in a strange sweet tongue. Often I stood, too, watching them, and taking in the fragrance of rugs and spices and onions and sweetmeats. And sometimes, suddenly remembering, I would hurry away for fear the school-bell had gone.

In class, long after I settled down, the thoughts of this alley would return to me. I would recall certain stalls and certain beards and certain flashing eyes, and even some of the rugs that had been rolled out. The Indian women, too, with bracelets around their ankles and around their sun-browned arms flashed to my mind.

I thought of them. I saw them again looking shyly at me from under the shadow of the stores, their veils half hiding their faces. In my mind I could almost picture them laughing together and talking in that strange sweet tongue. And mostly the day would be quite old before the spell of the alley wore off my mind.

One morning I was much too early for school. I passed streetsweepers at work on Harris' Promenade and when I came to the High Street only one or two shop doors were open. I walked slowly, looking at the quietness and noticing some of the alleys that ran away to the backs of fences and walls and distant streets. I looked at the names of these alleys. Some were very funny. And I walked on anxiously so I could look a little longer at the dark, funny street.

As I walked it struck me that I did not know the name of that street. I laughed at myself. Always I had stood there looking along it and I did not know the name of it. As I drew near I kept my eyes on the wall of the corner shop. There was no sign on the wall. On getting there I looked at the other wall. There was a sign-plate upon it but the dust had gathered thickly there and whatever the sign said was hidden behind the dust.

I was disappointed. I looked along the alley which was only now beginning to get alive, and as the shop doors opened the enchantment of spice and onions and sweetmeats emerged. I looked at the wall again but there was nothing there to say what the street was called. Straining my eyes at the sign-plate I could make out a 'C' and an 'A' but farther along the dust had made one smooth surface of the plate and the wall.

'Stupes!' I said in disgust. I heard mild laughter, and as I looked before me I saw the man rolling out his rugs. There were two women beside him and they were talking together and they were laughing and I could see the women were pretending not to look at me. They were setting up a stall of sweetmeats and the man put down his rugs and took out something from a tray and put it into his mouth, looking back at me. Then they talked again in the strange tongue and laughed.

I stood there awhile. I knew they were talking about me. I was not afraid. I wanted to show them that I was not timid and that I would not run away. I moved a step or two nearer the wall. The smell rose up stronger now and they seemed to give the feelings of things splendoured and far away. I pretended I was looking at the wall but I stole glances at the merchants from the corners of my eyes. I watched the men in their loin-

72

cloths and the garments of the women were full and many-coloured and very exciting. The women stole glances at me and smiled to each other and ate of the sweetmeats they sold. The rug merchant spread out his rugs wide on the pavement and he looked at the beauty of their colours and seemed very proud. He, too, looked slyly at me.

I drew a little nearer because I was not afraid of them. There were many more stalls now under the stores. Some of the people turned off the High Street and came into this little alley and they bought little things from the merchants. The merchants held up the bales of cloth and matched them on to the people's clothes and I could see they were saying it looked very nice. I smiled at this and the man with the rugs saw me and smiled.

That made me brave. I thought of the word I knew in the strange tongue and when I remembered it I drew nearer.

'Salaam,' I said.

The rug merchant laughed aloud and the two women laughed aloud and I laughed, too. Then the merchant bowed low to me and replied, 'Salaam!'

This was very amusing for the two women. They talked together so I couldn't understand and then the fat one spoke.

'Wot wrang wid de warl?'

I was puzzled for a moment and then I said, 'Oh, it is the street sign. Dust cover it.'

'Street sign?' one said, and they covered their laughter with their veils.

'I can't read what street it is,' I said. 'What street this is?'

The rug merchant spoke to the women in the strange tongue and the three of them giggled and one of the women said, 'Every marning you stand up dey and you doe know what they carl here?'

'First time I come down here,' I said.

'Yes,' said the fat woman. Her face was big and friendly and she sat squat on the pavement. 'First time you wark down here but every marning you stop dey and watch we.'

I laughed.

'You see 'e laughing?' said the other. The rug merchant did

74

not say anything but he was very much amused.

'What you call this street?' I said. I felt very brave because I knew they were friendly to me, and I looked at the stalls, and the smell of the sweetmeats was delicious. There was barah, too, and chutney and dry channa, and in the square tin there was the wet yellow channa, still hot, the steam curling up from it.

The man took time to put down his rugs and then he spoke to me. 'This,' he said, talking slowly and making actions with his arms, 'from up dey to up dey is Calcatta Street.' He was very pleased with his explanation. He had pointed from the High Street end of the alley to the other end that ran darkly into the distance. The whole street was very long and dusty, and in the concrete drain there was no water and the brown peel of onions blew about when there was a little wind. Sometimes there was the smell of cloves in the air and sometimes the smell of oilcloth, but where I stood the smell of the sweetmeats was strongest and most delicious.

He asked, 'You like Calcatta Street?'

'Yes,' I said.

The two women laughed coyly and looked from one to the other.

'I have to go,' I said, '– school.'

'O you gwine to school?' the man said. He put down his rugs again. His loin-cloth was very tight around him. 'Well you could wark so,' he said, pointing away from the High Street end of the alley, 'and when you get up dey, turn so, and when you wark and wark, you'll meet the school.'

'Oh!' I said, surprised. I didn't know there was a way to school along this alley.

'You see?' he said, very pleased with himself.

'Yes,' I said.

The two women looked at him smiling and they seemed very proud the way he explained. I moved off to go, holding my books under my arm. The woman looked at me and they smiled in a sad, friendly way. I looked at the chutney and barah and channa and suddenly something occurred to me. I felt in my pockets and then I opened my books and looked

75

among the pages. I heard one of the women whisper – 'Taking larning. . . .' The other said, 'Aha. . . .' and I did not hear the rest of what she said. Desperately I turned the books down and shook them and the penny fell out rolling on the pavement. I grabbed it up and turned to the fat woman. For a moment I couldn't decide which, but the delicious smell of the yellow, wet channa softened my heart.

'A penny channa,' I said, 'wet.'

The woman bent over with the big spoon, took out a small paper bag, flapped it open, then crammed two or three spoonfuls of channa into it. Then she took up the pepper bottle.

'Pepper?'

'Yes,' I said, anxiously.

'Plenty?'

'Plenty.'

The fat woman laughed, pouring the pepper sauce with two or three pieces of red pepper skin falling on the channa.

'Good!' I said, licking my lips.

'You see?' said the other woman. She grinned widely, her gold teeth glittering in her mouth. 'You see 'e like plenty pepper?'

As I handed my penny I saw the long, brown fingers of the rug merchant stretching over my head. He handed a penny to the fat lady.

'Keep you penny in you pocket,' he grinned at me, 'an look out, you go reach to school late.'

I was very grateful about the penny. I slipped it into my pocket.

'You could wark so,' the man said, pointing up Calcutta Street, 'and turn so, and you'll come down by the school.'

'Yes,' I said, hurrying off.

The street was alive with people now. There were many more merchants with rugs and many more stalls of sweetmeats and other things. I saw bales of bright cloth matched up to ladies' dresses and I heard the ladies laugh and say it was good. I walked fast through the crowd. There were women with sarees calling out 'Ground-nuts! Parata!' and every here and there gramophones blared out Indian songs. I walked on with my heart full inside me. Sometimes I stood up to listen and then I walked on again. Then suddenly it came home to me it must be very late. The crowd was thick and the din spread right along Calcutta Street. I looked back to wave to my friends. They were far behind and the pavement was so crowded I could not see. I heard the car horns tooting and I knew that on the High Street it must be a jam session of traffic and people. It must be very late. I held my books in my hands, secured the paper bag of channa in my pocket, and with the warmth against my legs I ran pell-mell to school.

The Idealist

FRANK O'CONNOR

I don't know how it is about education, but it never seemed to do anything for me but get me into trouble.

Adventure stories weren't so bad, but as a kid I was very serious and preferred realism to romance. School stories were what I liked best, and, judged by our standards, these were romantic enough for anyone. The schools were English, so I suppose you couldn't expect anything else. They were always called 'the venerable pile,' and there was usually a ghost in them; they were built in a square that was called 'the quad,' and, according to the pictures, they were all clock-towers, spires, and pinnacles, like the lunatic asylum with us. The fellows in the stories were all good climbers, and got in and out of school at night on ropes made of knotted sheets. They dressed queerly; they wore long trousers, short, black jackets, and top hats. Whenever they did anything wrong they were given 'lines' in Latin. When it was a bad case, they were flogged and never showed any sign of pain; only the bad fellows, and they always said: 'Ow! Ow!'

Most of them were grand chaps who always stuck together and were great at football and cricket. They never told lies and wouldn't talk to anyone who did. If they were caught out and asked a point-blank question, they always told the truth, unless someone else was with them, and then even if they were to be expelled for it they wouldn't give his name, even if he was a thief, which, as a matter of fact, he frequently was. It was surprising in such good schools, with fathers who never gave less than five quid, the number of thieves there were. The fellows in our school hardly ever stole, though they only got a penny a week, and sometimes not even that, as when their fathers were on the booze and their mothers had to go to the pawn.

78

I worked hard at the football and cricket, though of course we never had a proper football and the cricket we played was with a hurley stick against a wicket chalked on some wall. The officers in the barrack played proper cricket, and on summer evenings I used to go and watch them, like one of the souls in Purgatory watching the joys of Paradise.

Even so, I couldn't help being disgusted at the bad way things were run in our school. Our 'venerable pile' was a red-brick building without tower or pinnacle a fellow could climb, and no ghost at all: we had no team, so a fellow, no matter how hard he worked, could never play for the school, and, instead of giving you 'lines,' Latin or any other sort, Murderer Moloney either lifted you by the ears or bashed you with a cane. When he got tired of bashing you on the hands he bashed you on the legs.

But these were only superficial things. What was really wrong was ourselves. The fellows sucked up to the masters and told them all that went on. If they were caught out in anything they tried to put the blame on someone else, even if it meant telling lies. When they were caned they snivelled and said it wasn't fair; drew back their hands as if they were terrified, so that the cane caught only the tips of their fingers, and then screamed and stood on one leg, shaking out their fingers in the hope of getting it counted as one. Finally they roared that their wrist was broken and crawled back to their desks with their hands squeezed under their armpits, howling. I mean you couldn't help feeling ashamed, imagining what chaps from a decent school would think if they saw it.

My own way to school led me past the barrack gate. In those peaceful days sentries never minded you going past the guard-room to have a look at the chaps drilling in the barrack square; if you came at dinnertime they even called you in and gave you plumduff and tea. Naturally, with such temptations I was often late. The only excuse, short of a letter from your mother, was to say you were at early Mass. The Murderer would never know whether you were or not, and if he did anything to you you could easily get him into trouble with the parish priest. Even as kids we knew who the real boss of the school was.

But after I started reading those confounded school stories I was never happy about saying I had been to Mass. It was a lie, and I knew that the chaps in the stories would have died sooner than tell it. They were all round me like invisible presences, and I hated to do anything which I felt they might disapprove of.

One morning I came in very late and rather frightened.

'What kept you till this hour, Delaney?' Murderer Moloney asked, looking at the clock.

I wanted to say I had been to Mass, but I couldn't. The invisible presences were all about me.

'I was delayed at the barrack, sir,' I replied in panic.

There was a faint titter from the class, and Moloney raised his brows in mild surprise. He was a big powerful man with fair hair and blue eyes and a manner that at times was deceptively mild.

'Oh, indeed,' he said, politely enough. 'And what delayed you?'

'I was watching the soldiers drilling, sir,' I said.

The class tittered again. This was a new line entirely for them.

'Oh,' Moloney said casually, 'I never knew you were such a military man. Hold out your hand!'

Compared with the laughter the slaps were nothing, and besides, I had the example of the invisible presences to sustain me. I did not flinch. I returned to my desk slowly and quietly without snivelling or squeezing my hands, and the Murderer looked after me, raising his brows again as though to indicate that this was a new line for him, too. But the others gaped and whispered as if I were some strange animal. At playtime they gathered about me, full of curiosity and excitement.

'Delaney, why did you say that about the barrack?'

'Because 'twas true,' I replied firmly. 'I wasn't going to tell him a lie.'

'What lie?'

'That I was at Mass.'

'Then couldn't you say you had to go on a message?'

'That would be a lie too.'

81

'Cripes, Delaney,' they said, 'you'd better mind yourself. The Murderer is in an awful wax. He'll massacre you.'

I knew that. I knew only too well that the Murderer's professional pride had been deeply wounded, and for the rest of the day I was on my best behaviour. But my best wasn't enough, for I underrated the Murderer's guile. Though he pretended to be reading, he was watching me the whole time.

'Delaney,' he said at last without raising his head from the book, 'was that you talking?'

"Twas, sir,' I replied in consternation.

The whole class laughed. They couldn't believe but that I was deliberately trailing my coat, and, of course, the laugh must have convinced him that I was. I suppose if people do tell you lies all day and every day, it soon becomes a sort of perquisite which you resent being deprived of.

'Oh,' he said, throwing down his book, 'we'll soon stop that.'

This time it was a tougher job, because he was really on his mettle. But so was I. I knew this was the testing-point for me, and if only I could keep my head I should provide a model for the whole class. When I had got through the ordeal without moving a muscle, and returned to my desk with my hands by my sides, the invisible presences gave me a great clap. But the visible ones were nearly as annoyed as the Murderer himself. After school half a dozen of them followed me down the school yard.

'Go on!' they shouted truculently. 'Shaping as usual!'

'I was not shaping.'

'You were shaping. You're always showing off. Trying to pretend he didn't hurt you – a blooming crybaby like you!'

'I wasn't trying to pretend,' I shouted, even then resisting the temptation to nurse my bruised hands. 'Only decent fellows don't cry over every little pain like kids.'

'Go on!' they bawled after me. 'You ould idiot!' And, as I went down the school lane, still trying to keep what the stories called 'a stiff upper lip,' and consoling myself with the thought that my torment was over until next morning, I heard their mocking voices after me.

'Loony Larry! Yah, Loony Larry!'

I realized that if I was to keep on terms with the invisible presences I should have to watch my step at school.

So I did, all through that year. But one day an awful thing happened. I was coming in from the yard, and in the porch outside our schoolroom I saw a fellow called Gorman taking something from a coat on the rack. I always described Gorman to myself as 'the black sheep of the school.' He was a fellow I disliked and feared; a handsome, sulky, spoiled, and sneering lout. I paid no attention to him because I had escaped for a few moments into my dream-world in which fathers never gave less than fivers and the honour of the school was always saved by some quiet, unassuming fellow like myself – 'a dark horse,' as the stories called him.

'Who are you looking at?' Gorman asked threateningly.

'I wasn't looking at anyone,' I replied with an indignant start.

'I was only getting a pencil out of my coat,' he added, clenching his fists.

'Nobody said you weren't,' I replied, thinking that this was a very queer subject to start a row about.

'You'd better not, either,' he snarled. 'You can mind your own business.'

'You mind yours!' I retorted, purely for the purpose of saving face. 'I never spoke to you at all.'

And that, so far as I was concerned, was the end of it.

But after playtime the Murderer, looking exceptionally serious, stood before the class, balancing a pencil in both hands.

'Everyone who left the classroom this morning, stand out!' he called. Then he lowered his head and looked at us from under his brows. 'Mind now, I said everyone!'

I stood out with the others, including Gorman. We were all very puzzled.

'Did you take anything from a coat on the rack this morning?' the Murderer asked, laying a heavy, hairy paw on Gorman's shoulder and staring menacingly into his eyes.

'Me, sir?' Gorman exclaimed innocently. 'No, sir.'

'Did you see anyone else doing it?'

'No, sir.'

'You?' he asked another lad, but even before he reached me at all I realized why Gorman had told the lie and wondered frantically what I should do.

'You?' he asked me, and his big red face was close to mine, his blue eyes were only a few inches away, and the smell of his toilet soap was in my nostrils. My panic made me say the wrong thing as though I had planned it.

'I didn't take anything, sir,' I said in a low voice.

'Did you see someone else do it?' he asked, raising his brows and showing quite plainly that he had noticed my evasion. 'Have you a tongue in your head?' he shouted suddenly, and the whole class, electrified, stared at me. 'You?' he added curtly to the next boy as though he had lost interest in me.

'No, sir.'

'Back to your desks, the rest of you!' he ordered. 'Delaney, you stay here.'

He waited till everyone was seated again before going on.

'Turn out your pockets.'

I did, and a half-stifled giggle rose, which the Murderer quelled with a thunderous glance. Even for a small boy I had pockets that were museums in themselves: the purpose of half the things I brought to light I couldn't have explained myself. They were antiques, prehistoric and unlabelled. Among them was a school story borrowed the previous evening from a queer fellow who chewed paper as if it were gum. The Murderer reached out for it, and holding it at arm's length, shook it out with an expression of deepening disgust as he noticed the nibbled corners and margins.

'Oh,' he said disdainfully, 'so this is how you waste your time! What do you do with this rubbish – eat it?'

''Tisn't mine, sir,' I said against the laugh that sprang up. 'I borrowed it.'

'Is that what you did with the money?' he asked quickly, his fat head on one side.

'Money?' I repeated in confusion. 'What money?'

'The shilling that was stolen from Flanagan's overcoat this morning.'

(Flanagan was a little hunchback whose people coddled him; no one else in the school would have possessed that much money.)

'I never took Flanagan's shilling,' I said, beginning to cry, 'and you have no right to say I did.'

'I have the right to say you're the most impudent and defiant puppy in the school,' he replied, his voice hoarse with rage, 'and I wouldn't put it past you. What else can anyone expect and you reading this dirty, rotten, filthy rubbish?' And he tore my school story in halves and flung them to the furthest corner of the classroom. 'Dirty, filthy, English rubbish! Now, hold out your hand.'

This time the invisible presences deserted me. Hearing themselves described in these contemptuous terms, they fled. The Murderer went mad in the way people do whenever they're up against something they don't understand. Even the other fellows were shocked, and, heaven knows, they had little sympathy with me.

'You should put the police on him,' they advised me later in the playground. 'He lifted the cane over his shoulder. He could get the gaol for that.'

'But why didn't you say you didn't see anyone?' asked the eldest, a fellow called Spillane.

'Because I did,' I said, beginning to sob all over again at the memory of my wrongs. 'I saw Gorman.'

'Gorman?' Spillane echoed incredulously. 'Was it Gorman took Flanagan's money? And why didn't you say so?'

'Because it wouldn't be right,' I sobbed.

'Why wouldn't it be right?'

'Because Gorman should have told the truth himself,' I said. 'And if this was a proper school he'd be sent to Coventry.'

'He'd be sent where?'

'Coventry. No one would ever speak to him again.'

'But why would Gorman tell the truth if he took the money?' Spillane asked as you'd speak to a baby. 'Jay, Delaney,' he added pityingly, 'you're getting madder and madder. Now, look at what you're after bringing on yourself!'

Suddenly Gorman came lumbering up, red and angry.

'Delaney,' he shouted threateningly, 'did you say I took Flanagan's money?'

Gorman, though I of course didn't realize it, was as much at sea as Moloney and the rest. Seeing me take all that punishment rather than give him away, he concluded that I must be more afraid of him than of Moloney, and that the proper thing to do was to make me more so. He couldn't have come at a time when I cared less for him. I didn't even bother to reply but lashed out with all my strength at his brutal face. This was the last thing he expected. He screamed, and his hand came away from his face, all blood. Then he threw off his satchel and came at me, but at the same moment a door opened behind us and a lame teacher called Murphy emerged. We all ran like mad and the fight was forgotten.

It didn't remain forgotten, though. Next morning after prayers the Murderer scowled at me.

'Delaney, were you fighting in the yard after school yesterday?'

For a second or two I didn't reply. I couldn't help feeling that it wasn't worth it. But before the invisible presences fled forever, I made another effort.

'I was, sir,' I said, and this time there wasn't even a titter. I was out of my mind. The whole class knew it and was awestricken.

'Who were you fighting?'

'I'd sooner not say, sir,' I replied, hysteria beginning to well up in me. It was all very well for the invisible presences, but they hadn't to deal with the Murderer.

'Who was he fighting with?' he asked lightly, resting his hands on the desk and studying the ceiling.

'Gorman, sir,' replied three or four voices – as easy as that!

'Did Gorman hit him first?'

'No, sir. He hit Gorman first.'

'Stand out,' he said, taking up the cane. 'Now,' he added, going up to Gorman, 'you take this and hit him. And make sure you hit him hard,' he went on, giving Gorman's arm an encouraging squeeze. 'He thinks he's a great fellow. You show him now what we think of him.'

Gorman came towards me with a broad grin. He thought it a great joke. The class thought it a great joke. They began to roar with laughter. Even the Murderer permitted himself a modest grin at his own cleverness.

'Hold out your hand,' he said to me.

I didn't. I began to feel trapped and a little crazy.

'Hold out your hand, I say,' he shouted, beginning to lose his temper.

'I will not,' I shouted back, losing all control of myself.

'You what?' he cried incredulously, dashing at me round the classroom with his hand raised as though to strike me. 'What's that you said, you dirty little thief?'

'I'm not a thief, I'm not a thief,' I screamed. 'And if he comes near me I'll kick the shins off him. You have no right to give him that cane, and you have no right to call me a thief either. If you do it again, I'll go down to the police and then we'll see who the thief is.'

'You refused to answer my questions,' he roared, and if I had been in my right mind I should have known he had suddenly taken fright; probably the word 'police' had frightened him.

'No,' I said through my sobs, 'and I won't answer them now either. I'm not a spy.'

'Oh,' he retorted with a sarcastic sniff, 'so that's what you call a spy, Mr Delaney?'

'Yes, and that's what they all are, all the fellows here – dirty spies! – but I'm not going to be a spy for you. You can do your own spying.'

'That's enough now, that's enough!' he said, raising his fat hand almost beseechingly. 'There's no need to lose control of yourself, my dear young fellow, and there's no need whatever to screech like that. 'Tis most unmanly. Go back to your seat now and I'll talk to you another time.'

I obeyed, but I did no work. No one else did much either. the hysteria had spread to the class. I alternated between fits of exultation at my own successful defiance of the Murderer, and panic at the prospect of his revenge; and at each change of mood I put my face in my hands and sobbed again. The

Murderer didn't even order me to stop. He didn't so much as look at me.

After that I was the hero of the school for the whole afternoon. Gorman tried to resume the fight, but Spillane ordered him away contemptuously – a fellow who had taken the master's cane to another had no status. But that wasn't the sort of hero I wanted to be. I preferred something less sensational.

Next morning I was in such a state of panic that I didn't know how I should face school at all. I dawdled, between two minds as to whether or not I should mitch. The silence of the school lane and yard awed me. I had made myself late as well.

'What kept you, Delaney?' the Murderer asked quietly.

I knew it was no good.

'I was at Mass, sir.'

'All right. Take your seat.'

He seemed a bit surprised. What I had not realized was the incidental advantage of our system over the English one. By this time half a dozen of his pets had brought the Murderer the true story of Flanagan's shilling, and if he didn't feel a monster he probably felt a fool.

But by that time I didn't care. In my school sack I had another story. Not a school story this time, though. School stories were a washout. 'Bang! Bang!' – that was the only way to deal with men like the Murderer. 'The only good teacher is a dead teacher.'

The Night the Ghost Got In

JAMES THURBER

The ghost that got into our house on the night of November 17, 1915, raised such a hullabaloo of misunderstandings that I am sorry I didn't just let it keep on walking, and go to bed. Its advent caused my mother to throw a shoe through a window of the house next door and ended up with my grandfather shooting a patrolman. I am sorry, therefore, as I have said, that I ever paid any attention to the footsteps.

They began about a quarter past one o'clock in the morning, a rhythmic, quick-cadenced walking around the dining-room table. My mother was asleep in one room upstairs, my brother Herman in another; grandfather was in the attic, in the old walnut bed which, as you will remember, once fell on my father. I had just stepped out of the bathtub and was busily rubbing myself with a towel when I heard the steps. They were the steps of a man walking rapidly around the dining-room table downstairs. The light from the bathroom shone down the back steps, which dropped directly into the dining-room; I could see the faint shine of plates on the plate-rail; I couldn't see the table. The steps kept going round and round the table; at regular intervals a board creaked, when it was trod upon. I supposed at first that it was my father or my brother Roy, who had gone to Indianapolis but were expected home at any time. I suspected next that it was a burglar. It did not enter my mind until later that it was a ghost.

After the walking had gone on for perhaps three minutes, I tiptoed to Herman's room. 'Psst!' I hissed in the dark, shaking him. 'Awp,' he said, in the low, hopeless tone of a despondent beagle – he always half suspected that something would 'get him' in the night. I told him who I was. 'There's something downstairs!' I said. He got up and followed me to the head of the back staircase. We listened together. There was no sound.

89

The steps had ceased. Herman looked at me in some alarm: I had only the bath towel around my waist. He wanted to go back to bed, but I gripped his arm. 'There's something down there!' I said. Instantly the steps began again, circled the dining-room table like a man running, and started up the stairs towards us, heavily, two at a time. The light still shone palely down the stairs; we saw nothing coming; we only heard the steps. Herman rushed to his room and slammed the door. I slammed shut the door at the stairs top and held my knee against it. After a long minute, I slowly opened it again. There was nothing there. There was no sound. None of us ever heard the ghost again.

The slamming of the doors had aroused mother: she peered out of her room. 'What on earth are you boys doing?' she demanded. Herman ventured out of his room. 'Nothing,' he said, gruffly, but he was, in colour, a light green. 'What was all that running around downstairs?' said mother. So she had heard the steps, too! We just looked at her. 'Burglars!' she shouted intuitively. I tried to quiet her by starting lightly downstairs.

'Come on, Herman,' I said.

'I'll stay with mother,' he said. 'She's all excited.'

I stepped back onto the landing.

'Don't either of you go a step,' said mother. 'We'll call the police.' Since the phone was downstairs, I didn't see how we were going to call the police – nor did I want the police – but mother made one of her quick, incomparable decisions. She flung up a window of her bedroom which faced the bedroom windows of the house of a neighbour, picked up a shoe, and whammed it through a pane of glass across the narrow space that separated the two houses. Glass tinkled into the bedroom occupied by a retired engraver named Bodwell and his wife. Bodwell had been for some years in rather a bad way and was subject to mild 'attacks'. Most everybody we knew or lived near had *some* kind of attacks.

It was now about two o'clock of a moonless night; clouds hung black and low. Bodwell was at the window in a minute, shouting, frothing a little, shaking his fist. 'We'll sell the house and go back to Peoria,' we could hear Mrs Bodwell saying. It was some time before mother 'got through' to Bodwell. 'Burglars!' she shouted. 'Burglars in the house!' Herman and I hadn't dared to tell her that it was not burglars but ghosts, for she was even more afraid of ghosts than of burglars. Bodwell at first thought that she meant there were burglars in his house, but finally he quieted down and called the police for us over an extension phone by his bed. After he had disappeared from the window, mother suddenly made as if to throw another shoe, not because there was further need of it but, as she later explained, because the thrill of heaving a shoe through a window glass had enormously taken her fancy. I prevented her.

The police were on hand in a commendably short time: a Ford sedan full of them, two on motorcycles, and a patrol wagon with about eight in it and a few reporters. They began banging at our front door. Flashlights shot streaks of gleam up and down the walls, across the yard, down the walk between our house and Bodwell's. 'Open up!' cried a hoarse voice. 'We're men from Headquarters!' I wanted to go down and let them in, since there they were, but mother wouldn't hear of it. 'You haven't a stitch on,' she pointed out. 'You'd catch your death.' I wound the towel around me again. Finally the cops put their shoulders to our big heavy front door with its thick bevelled glass and broke it in: I could hear a rending of wood and a splash of glass on the floor of the hall. Their lights played all over the living-room and crisscrossed nervously in the dining-room, stabbed into hallways, shot up the front stairs and finally up the back. They caught me standing in my towel at the top. A heavy policeman bounded up the steps. 'Who are you?' he demanded. 'I live here,' I said. 'Well, whattsa matta, ya hot?' he asked. It was, as a matter of fact, cold; I went to my room and pulled on some trousers. On my way out, a cop stuck a gun into my ribs. 'Whatta you doin' here?' he demanded. 'I live here.' I said.

The officer in charge reported to mother. 'No sign of nobody, lady,' he said. 'Musta got away – whatt'd he look like?' 'There were two or three of them,' mother said, 'whooping and carrying on and slamming doors.' 'Funny,' said the cop. 'All ya windows and doors was locked on the inside right as a tick.'

Downstairs, we could hear the tromping of the other police. Police were all over the place; doors were yanked open, drawers were yanked open, windows were shot up and pulled down, furniture fell with dull thumps. A half-dozen policemen emerged out of the darkness of the front hallway upstairs. They began to ransack the floor: pulled beds away from walls, tore clothes off hooks in the closets, pulled suitcases and boxes off shelves. One of them found an old zither that Roy had won in a pool tournament. 'Looky here, Joe,' he said strumming it with a big paw. The cop named Joe took it and turned it over. 'What is it?' he asked me. 'It's an old zither our guinea pig used to sleep on,' I said. It was true that a pet guinea pig we once had would never sleep anywhere except on the zither but I should never have said so. Joe and the other cop looked at me a long time. They put the zither back on a shelf.

'No sign o' nuthin',' said the cop who had first spoken to mother. 'This guy,' he explained to the others, jerking a thumb at me, 'was nekked. The lady seems historical.' They all nodded, but said nothing; just looked at me. In the small silence we all heard a creaking in the attic. Grandfather was turning over in bed. 'What's 'at?' snapped Joe. Five or six cops sprang for the attic door before I could intervene or explain. I realized that it would be bad if they burst in on grandfather unannounced, or even announced. He was going through a phase in which he believed that General Meade's men, under steady hammering by Stonewall Jackson, were beginning to retreat and even desert.

When I got to the attic, things were pretty confused. Grandfather had evidently jumped to the conclusion that the police were deserters from Meade's army, trying to hide away in his attic. He bounded out of bed wearing a long flannel nightgown over long woollen underwear, a nightcap, and a leather jacket around his chest. The cops must have realized at once that the indignant white-haired old man belonged in the house, but they had no chance to say so. 'Back, ye cowardly dogs!' roared grandfather. 'Back t' the lines, ye goddam lily-livered cattle!' With that, he fetched the officer who found the zither a flat-handed smack alongside his head that sent him sprawling. The others beat a retreat, but not fast enough; grandfather grabbed Zither's gun from its holster and let fly. The report seemed to crack the rafters; smoke filled the attic. A cop cursed and shot his hand to his shoulder. Somehow, we all finally got downstairs again and locked the door against the old gentleman. He fired once or twice more in the darkness and then went back to bed. 'That was grandfather,' I explained to Joe, out of breath. 'He thinks you're deserters.' 'I'll say he does,' said Joe.

The cops were reluctant to leave without getting their hands on somebody besides grandfather; the night had been distinctly a defeat for them. Furthermore, they obviously didn't like the 'layout'; something looked – and I can see their viewpoint – phony. They began to poke into things again. A reporter, a thin-faced, wispy man, came up to me. I had put on one of mother's blouses, not being able to find anything else. The reporter looked at me with mingled suspicion and interest. 'Just what the hell is the real lowdown here, Bud?' he asked. I decided to be frank with him. 'We had ghosts,' I said. He gazed at me a long time as if I were a slot machine into which he had, without results, dropped a nickel. Then he walked away. The cops followed him, the one grandfather shot holding his now-bandaged arm, cursing and blaspheming. 'I'm gonna get my gun back from that old bird,' said the zither-cop. 'Yeh,' said Joe. 'You – and who else?' I told them I would bring it to the station house next day.

'What was the matter with that one policeman?' mother asked, after they had gone. 'Grandfather shot him,' I said. 'What for?' she demanded. I told her he was a deserter. 'Of all things!' said mother. 'He was such a nice-looking young man.'

Grandfather was fresh as a daisy and full of jokes at breakfast next morning. We thought at first he had forgotten all about what had happened, but he hadn't. Over his third cup of coffee, he glared at Herman and me. 'What was the idee of all them cops tarryhootin' round the house last night?' he demanded. He had us there.

Follow On

Casey and the Damp Squibs

About the Story

This story describes the attempts of a group of Liverpool children to earn enough money to buy fireworks. They are very much city children – lively and cheerful, living in the streets, getting into mischief, but doing no real harm to anyone. They live very much in a world of their own and generally treat adults with scorn or indifference – though they sometimes have their uses.

For Discussion or Writing

1. What can we tell about the characters in the story from their names?
2. What really upsets Tommy Mac and his friends about not having enough money to buy fireworks?
3. Describe the behaviour of the gang in the snack bar.
4. Why does the gang dislike school?
5. What do we learn about the place the gang lives in and about the other people who live there?
6. What is Tommy Mac's attitude towards pricing and selling his goods?
7. Comment on Constable Jackson's treatment of the boys.
8. Explain the reasons given by Tommy's father and mother for going to the Corporation's firework display.
9. Why does Casey scorn this?
10. Describe the scene at the official firework display.
11. Why is Tommy Mac's gang so delighted at the end of the story?
12. What is your reaction to the way the story ends?

For Writing

1. Look at the various adults the members of the gang come in contact with and describe what the gang's feelings are towards them.

2. Write an account of what happens in the story from the point of view of Casey.
3. Write another story about Tommy Mac and his friends.
4. Have you ever tried to earn some money by doing or making something? Write about it.
5. Write a story about Fireworks Night.

Further Reading
'Casey and the Damp Squibs' is just one of a number of stories by Margaret Stuart Barry about Tommy Mac and his friends. The author herself teaches in a Liverpool school so she knows the people she is writing about. If you enjoyed this story, try to read some more. They can be found in *Tommy Mac*, *Tommy Mac Battles On* and *Tommy Mac on Safari*.

What the Neighbours Did

About the Story
We are not told where this story is set, but it seems to be a much more rural setting than 'Casey and the Damp Squibs'. The story is about how you can't help overhearing what goes on in the lives of your neighbours and getting involved – even if you don't particularly want to.

For Discussion or Writing
1. Describe how Mrs Macy treats her husband.
2. Why does the boy's dad get annoyed when the boy keeps asking him what would happen to the dog?
3. Why is Mr Macy so anxious to know whether Dirty Dick had told the police about the theft of his money?
4. What is Dirty Dick's reaction to the theft?
5. Why should Mr Macy feel spiteful towards Dirty Dick?
6. Why do you think the boy in the story envies Dirty Dick?
7. Why is his mother angry at him for this?
8. Why do you think Dirty Dick left?

For Writing
1. Outline the part played in the story by the blind dog.
2. Write a description of Dirty Dick and the kind of life he leads.

3. Write about your own neighbours.
4. Write a story in which you get into trouble with the neighbours or in which you are able to help your neighbours.

Further Reading

Philippa Pearce is a well-known writer of books for young people. Her novel *Tom's Midnight Garden* has been described – with much justification – as one of the most perfect books ever written for young people. She writes about seemingly ordinary things with humour and understanding. Further short stories by her can be found in the volume called *What the Neighbours Did* and in *The Shadow-Cage* which is a collection of stories of the supernatural. Try to read them. Novels by Philippa Pearce that you would enjoy are *The Minnow on the Say*, *A Dog So Small*, *The Children of the House* (written with Brian Fairfax-Lucy) and, of course, *Tom's Midnight Garden*.

A Bit of Bread and Jam

About the Story

Another hen-pecked husband is at the bottom of the events in this story (as in 'What the Neighbours Did'), but it has more in common with 'Casey and the Damp Squibs' – a story about a group of lads and how they spend their time. It is set in Lancashire about fifty years ago, though the kind of near-disaster described in the story could just as easily happen today.

For Discussion or Writing

1. Why are the boys reluctant to go on an errand for Mrs Hoskey?
2. Why does Billy finally agree?
3. How does Mrs Hoskey treat her husband?
4. What so surprises Billy about Felix's behaviour at the river bank?
5. Why does Felix behave like this?
6. What is the difference in atmosphere and appearance between Pike's lodge and Pratt and Dyson's lodge?
7. How does Billy react to the others when he catches his first carp?

8. Why does Billy not share his bait with the others?
9. Explain why Billy's bait was so successful.
10. Why does Billy at the end not care whether 'they'd fuss me at home or give me a good hiding'?

For Writing
1. Write an account of Mrs Hoskey, describing everything we learn about the kind of person she is, how she treats her husband, what other people think of her, and what happens to her.
2. Compare the personality and behaviour of Mr Hoskey with those of Mr Macy in 'What the Neighbours Did'.
3. Write a story about a group of friends who get involved in a game that goes wrong.
4. The Narrow Escape. Write a story about someone who narrowly escapes death.
5. Write a fishing story about 'the one that got away'.

Further Reading
Bill Naughton was born in Ireland in 1910 but was brought up in Lancashire. He spent many years in tough jobs, often being out of work, before he became a successful writer of books and plays like *Alfie, Spring and Port Wine* and *All in Good Time*. Much of his writing is loosely autobiographical, that is, based on his own memories and experiences. If you enjoyed 'A Bit of Bread and Jam', you would like the other stories in the book it comes from, *The Goalkeeper's Revenge*. *My Pal Spadger* and *A Dog Called Nelson* are two other books by Bill Naughton you would enjoy. More directly autobiographical are *A Roof Over Your Head* and *One Small Boy* which describe the hard times (and pleasures) many people had forty or fifty years ago. Older readers would appreciate the short stories in *Late Night on Watling Street*.

The Apple of Trouble

About the Story
This story is clearly meant to be taken with a pinch of salt. It is a comic fantasy in which all kinds of impossible and absurd things happen. The way in which the characters react to these

events, and the way in which the author tells the story increase the comic effect. Towards the end, events pile up on top of each other with hilarious results.

For Discussion or Writing

1. What signs are there at the beginning of the story that it is not to be taken too seriously?
2. How does Uncle Gavin's behaviour indicate that he was once a High Commissioner?
3. How does Mark react when he is first shown the apple?
4. Why is the foreign-looking man so eager to exchange the apple?
5. Can you explain the references to the apple's previous history?
6. What kind of 'spelling' is Harriet learning?
7. Why is Uncle Gavin being so pleasant at the end of the story?
8. Mark and Harriet remained unsurprised no matter what happens. Give some examples of the unusual things that occur in the story and try to explain why the children's calm acceptance of them increases the comedy.
9. Describe an incident in the story that you found particularly amusing.
10. Some of the comedy lies in the way the author turns a phrase or says something unexpected. Can you find examples?

For Writing

1. Write an account of Uncle Gavin and his behaviour.
2. Write about what makes this story comic.
3. Write a story about an unwelcome relation who comes to stay.
4. Write a story about a spell that works or a spell that goes wrong.

Further Reading

As you will realise from reading 'The Apple of Trouble', Joan Aiken is a writer with a very vivid imagination. Anything and everything can happen in her stories and novels. Wolves can still be roaming England, for instance, and James III can be on the throne. Not everyone will appreciate her sense of humour and delight in fantasy, but if you enjoyed 'The Apple of Trouble', try some of the other stories in *A Small Pinch of Weather, All and More, A Necklace of Raindrops* and *All You've Ever Wanted*. Novels by Joan Aiken you may enjoy are *The Wolves of Willoughby Chase, Black Hearts in Battersea, Night Birds on Nantucket, The Whispering Mountain, The Cuckoo Tree* and *Midnight is a Place*.

Memories of Christmas

About the Story

Dylan Thomas gives an impression of what Christmas was like when he was young with detail piled on detail and all the Christmases that ever were rolled into one. The story describes the excitement and the presents, the adventures and food, the stories and the atmosphere in a great rush of words and images and events. Dylan Thomas was a poet and 'Memories of Christmas' was originally given by him as a radio talk on *Children's Hour*. Both of these facts affect the way the story is written.

For Discussion or Writing

1. Dylan Thomas says that when he was young 'one Christmas was so much like another'. Pick out some of the things he remembers.
2. What impression of his neighbours and family does the young Dylan Thomas give?
3. Pick out some details from the story which show that Dylan and his friends had vivid imaginations.
4. How old do you think Dylan and his friends are? Why?
5. Do you think Dylan Thomas gives a convincing account of the way children of that age think, speak and behave?
6. Dylan Thomas uses words in an interesting way. Pick out some examples that are particularly notable.
7. Can you point to any things in the story which show that it was originally a radio talk?

For Writing

1. Write about the way Dylan Thomas uses words and comparisons in this story.

99

2. Write about your memories of Christmas.
3. Write a story about a group of people going carol singing.
4. Write a Christmas ghost story.

Further Reading
Dylan Thomas was born in Swansea in 1914 and died at the early age of thirty-nine. He achieved considerable fame for his rich and colourful poetry and his bohemian life. You may enjoy some of the other stories and sketches in *Quite Early One Morning* and in *Portrait of the Artist as a Young Dog*. Older readers would appreciate Dylan Thomas' radio play *Under Milk Wood* and would find many of his poems rewarding to study.

The Lumber-Room

About the Story
This story indicates clearly that children and adults have very different kinds of minds and very different ways of looking at things. By showing how easy it is for Nicholas to hoodwink his aunt and make a fool of her, the author is making fun of this narrow-minded, rather stupid kind of person. The story is set in the days more than sixty years ago when it was not uncommon for well-off families to have servants and nurseries and large gardens.

For Discussion or Writing
1. Why does Nicholas lose faith in the superiority of adults?
2. How does the aunt deal with one or other of the children when they disgrace themselves?
3. Judging from how they set out, do you think the other children are likely to enjoy their outing to Jagborough?
4. Why does Nicholas pretend that he wants to get into the gooseberry garden?
5. Why does Nicholas find the lumber-room interesting and exciting?
6. Explain how Nicholas turns the tables on his aunt.

For Writing
1. Outline the various stages in the battle between Nicholas and his aunt.

2. Imagine that you are Nicholas and write down his views on adults.
3. Write a story in which a child is punished for being naughty.
4. Write a story in which a child manages to get the better of an adult.

Further Reading
Saki was the pen-name of H. H. Munro who was born in 1870 and was killed in 1916 during the First World War. He was a master of the short story. His stories are witty and make fun of the attitudes and snobberies of Edwardian society. They are rather like the rude but clever comments an upper-class school-boy might make about his so-called superiors. They were written for adults and require close attention from the reader if they are to be fully appreciated. If you liked 'The Lumber-Room', you could try some of the others. There is a collected edition.

The Doll's House

About the Story
This story shows how cruel children can be to other children. But it also shows how the attitudes and opinions of parents and adults can be conveyed to children and how easily children imitate these attitudes. It is possible to say that the Burnell children and the others are not being naturally unpleasant to the Kelveys: they are merely behaving in the way that their parents expect and want them to behave. The story was written about the same time as 'The Lumber-Room' by Saki when some children led very privileged lives with servants and large houses.

For Discussion or Writing
1. Contrast the different attitudes towards the doll's house held by Aunt Beryl and the children.
2. What do the Burnells feel about the school they have to send their children to?
3. Why were the two Kelvey children rejected by all the others?
4. Describe the two Kelvey children.

5. Why does Lena's taunt that Lil would be a servant when she grows up fall flat?
6. Why do you think Kezia invited the Kelveys to see the doll's house?
7. Why is Aunt Beryl so angry?
8. Whom do you feel sorry for in this story and why?

For Writing
1. Write an account of the events of the story as if you were Lil or our Else.
2. Children can often be very cruel to each other. Write down your views on this statement giving as many examples as you can supporting or rejecting it.
3. Write a story in which a child or a group of children taunt or torment another child.
4. Write a story about someone being given a splendid present and about what he or she does with it.

Further Reading
Katherine Mansfield was born in New Zealand in 1888. She developed tuberculosis and died in 1923. Most of her writing took the form of short stories, and many of these (including 'The Doll's House') are based on her memories of her childhood in New Zealand. Katherine Mansfield was writing for adult readers, but you would find many of her stories interesting. They show a deep understanding of how people think and behave. Try to read some more of them. There is a collected edition.

Enchanted Alley

About the Story
There is very little 'plot' in this story. It is simply an account of a boy noticing, as though for the first time, an alley with mysterious shops and rich goods and exotic smells. Although so ordinary, the story represents an important moment in the author's life – the moment when he first really looked at people and places. The story is set in San Fernando in Trinidad. 'Channa' is a kind of chutney.

For Discussion or Writing
1. What do you think it is about the alley that so attracts the writer?
2. What is the attitude of the men and women of the alley towards the writer?
3. Much of the appeal of the alley is an appeal to the senses of sight and hearing and smell. Pick out details.
4. What do you learn about the character of the writer from this story?
5. The writer is black of African descent; the merchants and their families are of Indian descent. Does this have any effect on the meaning of the story?

For Writing
1. Write an account of the activity going on in the alley.
2. Write about the food you like and dislike.
3. Write a description of a street you know well. It could be your own street, a street market or a busy High Street.
4. Write about the journey you make to school every morning. Give plenty of detail and try to describe things you pass or notice as though you are seeing them for the first time.

Further Reading
Michael Anthony was born in Trinidad in 1932. Much of his writing is about growing up on that island. If you enjoyed this story, try to read other stories in the collection *Cricket in the Road*. The story 'Enchanted Alley' contains the idea which was later expanded into the novel *The Year in San Fernando* which you would also find interesting. Older readers should also consider Michael Anthony's novels *The Games Were Coming* and *Green Days by the River*.

The Idealist

About the Story
This story is set in Ireland about sixty years ago. On the face of it, life for the hero and his friends was hard and the events described in the story are grim. Nevertheless, a kind of chirpy humour keeps breaking through, and the reader can't help

feeling that the hero will survive. The story provides an opportunity to compare the attitudes of teachers and pupils then with those of today.

For Discussion or Writing
1. Describe the kind of books the hero of this story enjoyed reading.
2. How does the life and behaviour of the characters in these books differ from that of the pupils at the hero's school? Which type seems to you more true to life?
3. What effect do these books have on the way the hero behaves?
4. What does the rest of the class think about this kind of behaviour?
5. When accused of theft, why does Delaney not tell the Murderer about Gorman?
6. Why does Delaney attack Gorman, and why is Gorman surprised?
7. How does Delaney turn the tables on the Murderer?
8. How does the rest of the class feel about Delaney now?
9. What effect does this have on Delaney's attitude towards lying?
10. Are you surprised at Delaney's views on teachers?
11. Do teachers today behave like the Murderer?
12. What are your views on the punishments used in schools?
13. What is an idealist? Explain why the story is called 'The Idealist'.

For Writing
1. Write an extract that could come from one of the school stories that Delaney so avidly reads.
2. Write a story in which a teacher and a pupil come into conflict (not necessarily physical! – it could be a disagreement).
3. Write a story about someone who is wrongfully accused of doing something.
4. Write about corporal punishment, giving both sides of the argument.

Further Reading

Ireland has produced a number of great writers of short stories, and Frank O'Connor is one of them. He was born in 1903 and died in 1966. He wrote with sympathy and understanding about how people behave towards each other, particularly in the small closely-knit communities that exist in Ireland. But his stories are not just about Irish people: they describe human behaviour anywhere. Try to read some more short stories by Frank O'Connor. They have been collected in *The Stories of Frank O'Connor*, *Collection Two* and *Collection Three*. Older readers may also find his autobiographies, *An Only Child* and *My Father's Son*, interesting.

The Night the Ghost Got In

About the Story

To outsiders, families can often seem to behave in rather odd ways, although the families themselves see nothing unusual in the kind of life they lead. In this story, James Thurber describes an event that happened in his own family. The comedy lies in the eccentric reactions to the events and the crazy logic of what happens, the bewilderment of the police, and the way in which one thing leads to another.

For Discussion or Writing

1. At what point does the author suspect that the footsteps belong to a ghost?
2. Why does Herman say he will stay with mother when the author begins to go downstairs?
3. Comment on some of the logical or illogical things the author's mother says.
4. What impression do the police get of the Thurber household?
5. Describe some of the odd behaviour the Thurber family indulges in.
6. What is comic about the ending of the story?

For Writing

1. Imagine the report the policemen make about the evening's events when they return to the police station.

2. Describe the Thurber family.
3. Outline the events of the story, showing how one thing leads to another.
4. Write a story about something strange or unusual that happened to your family.
5. Write a story describing what happens when one of your family imagines he hears a ghost.

Further Reading
James Thurber was born in Columbus, Ohio, in 1894 and died in 1961. He was one of America's greatest humorists. Much of his comic writing deals with his eccentric family or pets and the kind of life they led in his home town. If you would like to find out more about them, read *My Life and Hard Times*, or *Thurber's Dogs*, or the collection *The Thurber Carnival*.